AF531441

MARKETS AND AGRICULTURAL DEVELOPMENT

MARKETS AND AGRICULTURAL DEVELOPMENT

By

Dr. M. Lakshmi Narasaiah
M.A., Ph.D.

Professor of Economics,
Coordinator, Department of M.B.A.
Sri Krishnadevaraya University Post-graduate Centre,
Kurnool–518 002
Andhra Pradesh (India).

DISCOVERY PUBLISHING HOUSE
NEW DELHI

First Published–2005

ISBN: 81-7141-926-7

Published by:

DISCOVERY PUBLISHING HOUSE

4831/24, Prahlad Street, Ansari Road, Darya Ganj
New Delhi–110 002 (India)
Phone: 23279245, • Fax: 91-11-23253475
e-mail: dphtemp@indiatimes.com

Printed at:

Tarun Offset Printers,
Delhi-110 053

Preface

While the Uruguay Round made a good start—more was done to liberalize agricultural trade and to being agriculture into the system that in all previous rounds combined—we have to recognize that agriculture still has a long way to go to complete its reform and to be fully integrated into the world trading system. Prior to the Uruguay Round, agricultural trading rules were not in concert with other sectors. The Uruguay Round Agreement (URAA) made good first steps toward bringing agriculture into conformity with international trade rules governing other goods, but much remains to be done.

The Uruguay Round, of course, required certain reductions in trade-distorting measures, and the implementation of those reforms has proceeded very well. Two other legacies of the Uruguay Round are very important for the new negotiations—a mandate to continue what was begun, and a structure for achieving liberalisation. The WTO's "built-in" agenda includes agriculture. It was recognized from the outset that the first period of reform that we are still implementing was only a down payment.

In addition to the commitment to continue negotiations, the URAA—focusing on export subsidies, market access, and domestic support—established a structure on which to build. Establishing a three-pillar structure was the most time-consuming undertaking in the round. Fortunately, we do not need to reinvent that wheel. The structure of the rules provides a logical approach for the negotiations, one which most seem to agree we should keep and build on.

Export Competition

Export subsidies are an illegitimate policy instrument, a symptom of a systemic imbalance in a nation's agricultural policies, the costs of which reborne by others. The costs of domestic policy, choices should be borne by the country that chooses them, not foisted onto its trading partners by subsidizing exports. The Uruguay Round made a start at eliminating agricultural export subsidies: 36 per cent reduction of budget expenditures on export subsidies and 21 per cent reduction of quantities over a six-year implementation period. With experience to show that markets adapt, we should now be able to improve the pace of export subsidy reductions and eliminate the export subsidy scourge from agricultural trade. Export subsidies are not allowed in the WTO rules for any other industry. Their use constitutes a source of trade distortion and degradation to the environment, and there is no valid reason to keep them any longer.

Market Access

The Uruguay Round progress on market access leaves much to be done. It left tariffs too high, and it did not create much new market access. The average non-agricultural tariff is now 4 per cent, while the average agricultural tariff is over 40 per cent, and tariffs on some products exceed 300 per cent. With a few exceptions, nontariff barriers were converted to tariffs, and members were required to open up at least a small minimum access-3 per cent of domestic consumption initially, growing to 5 per cent by the end of the adjustment period—under tariff-rate quotas.

The stage has been set for real reforms. Let access continue to grow and let all tariffs be reduced to a negotiated maximum level by the end of the transition period. In addition, an examination of the administration of tariff-rate quotas should lead to transparent and open systems.

Many WTO members note that importers were required to change nontariff barriers to tariffs and grant access, while no reciprocal disciplines were imposed on export restraints of exporting countries. Net food importing countries should be able to expect that if they open their border to international market, those international markets will deliver supplies as reliably to importers as to the domestic markets of exporters. Willingness on the part of leading exporting members to discipline export controls will reassure "food security" countries that expanding market access is not risky.

Domestic Support

The Aggregate Measure of Support was a success as a component of the Agreement on Agriculture and the insistence on reducing trade-distorting measures. The drive toward decoupled support ("green box") is the key. By the end of 1996, the United States had largely decoupled farm programmes so that payments to farmers were not linked to a requirement to produce. Other WTO members will also succeed in orienting their policies toward market signals. In the new round, further review and decreases in the aggregate measure of support will clearly lead to market-based agricultural trade.

Dr. M. Lakshmi Narasaiah

Contents

1

Opening Markets for Agriculture

While the Uruguay Round made a good start—more was done to liberalize agricultural trade and to being agriculture into the system than in all previous rounds combined—we have to recognize that agriculture still has a long way to go to complete its reform and to be fully integrated into the world trading system. Prior to the Uruguay Round, agricultural trading rules were not in concert with other sectors. The Uruguay Round Agreement (URAA) made good first steps toward bringing agriculture into conformity with international trade rules governing other goods, but much remains to be done.

The Uruguay Round, of course, required certain reductions in trade-distorting measures, and the implementation of those reforms has proceeded very well. Two other legacies of the Uruguay Round are very important for the new negotiations—a mandate to continue what was begun, and a structure for achieving liberalisation. The WTO's "built-in" agenda includes agriculture. It was recognized from the outset that the first period of reform that we are still implementing was only a down payment.

In addition to the commitment to continue negotiations, the URAA—focusing on export subsidies, market access, and domestic support—established a structure on which to build. Establishing a three-pillar structure was the most time-consuming undertaking in the round. Fortunately, we do not need to reinvent that wheel. The structure of the rules provides a logical approach for the negotiations, one which most seem to agree we should keep and build on.

Export Competition

Export subsidies are an illegitimate policy instrument, a symptom of a systemic imbalance in a nation's agricultural policies, the costs of which reborne by others. The costs of domestic policy, choices should be borne by the country that chooses them, not foisted onto its trading partners by subsidizing exports. The Uruguay Round made a start at eliminating agricultural export subsidies: 36 per cent reduction of budget expenditures on export subsidies and 21 per cent reduction of quantities over a six-year implementation period. With experience to show that markets adapt, we should now be able to improve the pace of export subsidy reductions and eliminate the export subsidy scourge from agricultural trade. Export subsidies are not allowed in the WTO rules for any other industry. Their use constitutes a source of trade distortion and degradation to the environment, and there is no valid reason to keep them any longer.

Market Access

The Uruguay Round progress on market access leaves much to be done. It left tariffs too high, and it did not create much new market access. The average non-agricultural tariff is now 4 per cent, while the average agricultural tariff is over 40 per cent, and tariffs on some products exceed 300 per cent. With a few exceptions, nontariff barriers were converted to tariffs, and members were required to open up at least a small minimum acess-3 per cent of domestic consumption initially, growing to 5 per cent by the end of the adjustment period—under tariff-rate quotas.

The stage has been set for real reforms. Let access continue to grow and let all tariffs be reduced to a negotiated maximum level by the end of the transition period. In addition, an examination of the administration of tariff-rate quotas should lead to transparent and open systems.

Many WTO members note that importers were required nontariff brriers to tariffs and grant access, while no reciprocal disciplines were imposed on export restraints of exporting countries. Net food importing countries should be able to expect that if they open their border to international market, those international markets will deliver supplies as reliably to importers as to be domestic markets of exports. Willingness on the part of leading exporting members to discipline export controls will reassure "food security" countries that expanding market access is not risky.

Domestic Support

The Aggregate Measure of Support was a success as a component of the Agreement on Agriculture and the instance on reducing trade-distorting measures. The drive toward decoupled support ("green box") is the key. By the end of 1996, the United States had largely decoupled farm programmes so that payments to farmers were not linked to a requirement to produce. Other WTO members will also succeed in orienting their policies toward market signals. In the new round, further review and decreases in the aggregate measure of support will clearly lead to market-based agricultural trade.

A new buzzword that some countries are using to justify domestic support is "multi functionality". It is a buzzword for what everybody in agriculture has known for thousands of years: agriculture serves other purposes besides producing food and fiber. But the real problem with the discussion of multi-functionality is not semantic. It is the confusion between policy goals and policy instruments. If the United States appears skeptical about the implications of multi-functionality for WTO rules, the U.S. objection is not multi-functionality as a factual matter. Each country chooses social objectives for themselves. There is no inherent connection between those objectives and trade-distorting agricultural polices.

New Issues

While the Uruguay Round established effective disciplines in traditional problem areas, such disciplines have not yet been established in some new areas. As monopolies, state trading enterprises (STEs) can distort trade, and they frequently operate behind a veil of secrecy. The agricultural trading system has much to gain from WTO disciplines on

STEs because they allow some countries to undercut exports based on open market transactions and restrict imports.

Biotechnology holds tremendous promise globally for food consumers, producers, and the environment. With the world's population growing by about 2 per cent annually, there are 80 million more mouths to feed each year. Some countries threaten to adopt policies regarding the importation and planting of bio-engineered crops and the labelling of products containing bio-engineered foods that are not based on scientifically justified principles. If our farmers are to meet the challenge of feeding an ever-increasing population with a sustainable agricultural system, then they must have access to the new bio-engineered varieties. We need to think about how the WTO can help facilitate this new technology.

Developing Countries

One of the critical components to a successful new round of negotiations will be the full participation of a substantially increased number of developing countries. Open trade in agriculture relieves farmers in developing countries of the burden imposed by protectionism and export subsidies, while reducing hunger and offering reliable supplies of food at reasonable prices.

2

The Future of Agricultural Trade

In the Uruguay Round, countries recognised that the long term solution for agriculture did not lie in administered prices, trade restrictions, supply controls, and export subsidies but rather in open, nondistorted markets. It is the time take bold steps toward bringing agricultural trade into the 21st century by accelerating agricultural trade reform.

There are four key areas for accelerating reforms: eliminating export subsidies; increasing market access though substantial tariff cuts and expansion of tariff-rate quotas; cutting further trade-distorting domestic subsidies; and ensuring technical standards are based on sound science.

The world's farmers and ranchers are facing two difficult challenges at the dawn of the 21st century. First, they are being asked to provide more products at lower cost, higher quality, greater variety, and in a safer manner than ever demanded before. Second, they are being asked to produce this abundance on a shrinking natural resources base that is often subject to government regulations. Meeting these global challenges will require unleashing the production potential of world agriculture while practising proper environmental stewardship. The ingenuity and hardwork we usually associate with farmers will be essential to meet these challenges, but they will not be sufficient unless we further reform agricultural, trade to create an environment that rewards risk and investment and encourages efficiencies.

Today's Agricultural Challenges

Farmers are responsible for feeding a rapidly growing

world population. And despite progress over the years, too many people still are not getting enough food. Many countries including the United States, are working vigorously to promote technological innovations to meet the need for food and fiber in the coming years. However, as important as this work is, it is only part of the solution. These technologies and the hard work of the world's farmers need a trading environment that encourages investment and efficient production, and generates economic growth to finance production and consumption needs long-term trends in agriculture pose serious challenges for all farmers. The same technological advances that increase yields may result in lower prices. Increasing social concerns about effect of agricultural production on the environment and living conditions result in new restrictions on farm activities. As urban dwellers and industry stake competing claims for land, water, and energy, many producers find their ability to farm made ever more difficult.

Two approaches to organizing the agricultural economy present a stark contrast in dealing with these challenges. One model, popular in Europe and Asia, is to retain an inward-looking agricultural system focused on supply control and government regulation geared to keeping farm prices high and, since guaranteed high prices are a drain on the treasury, to controlling production. Under this approach, bureaucrats try to assess the optimal level of national production—not so little that imports are needed and not so much that excess production; must be bought at high prices and; then dumped on world markets. This "command-and-control" structure stifles farmer efficiency and ingenuity and distorts world markets, especially as subsidized surpluses are regularly exported; and it does not address the challenge to farmers to produce food for the next century. It also ignores the interest of domestic consumers (who have to pay high internal prices) and producers in other countries (who have to compete with subsidized products). Of biggest concern is that the anti-market policies of this approach hamstring the agriculture sector from pursuing the technological advances needed to meet its future challenges.

Another approach is to place agriculture on a more market-oriented basis, particularly by removing trade barriers and reducing trade-distorting policies. Greater market orientation was the principle that actions agreed to in the last set of multilateral trade negotiations. In the Uruguay Round, countries recognized that the long-term solution for agriculture did not lie in administered prices, trade restrictions, supply controls, and export subsidies but rather in open, nondistorted markets. Now is the time to take bold steps toward bringing agricultural trade into the 21st century by accelerating agricultural trade reform.

The Gains From Trade

The benefit from free and fair trading of agricultural products have immediate effects on people. Eliminating trade barriers and reducing unfair competition will help ensure that farmers have incentives to produce and consumers have access to the products they desire. Liberalizing agricultural trade will contribute to better resource allocation by farmers, which has conservation benefits, rewards low-cost producers, encourages efficiencies, and removes the drag on economic growth.

Opening trading opportunities also increases the food security of food-importing countries by giving supplier countries the confidence required to put more land into production and to create marketing relationships. Trade provides consumers with year-round access to a greater variety of less expensive products, while rewarding producers who are able to find and meet specific consumer demands for high-value products. In a broader context, by allowing imports that are more efficiently produced elsewhere, trade encourages specialisation in efficient agricultural and nonagricultural production.

More dramatically, trade literally saves lives. Without the international flow of food products from areas with abundant production to areas where food is scarce, many people in the world would be eating less or not at all. Trade has dynamic effects, as well, that push long-term productivity growth. For example, access to customers in overseas markets creates an incentive for technological innovation, resulting in exciting developments in improved seed varieties and production techniques. International markets also expand market outlets, raising prices and giving producers increased confidence to produce more than required merely for national needs, allowing productive farmers to not only feed their neighbours but literally feed the world.

Equally important, trade in agricultural products is becoming increasingly critical to farm and ranch incomes. Increased productivity and often times flat domestic demand increases the importance of reliable international markets. Foreign markets are not just a dumping ground for surplus products; overseas consumers value choice and quality, particularly when producers in their own country cannot meet their demands or when they are charged inflated prices. Consequently foreign and value-added agricultural producers, raising farm-gate prices and helping support the range of agriculture-related industries.

Political reality also encourages a focus on international markets; policies based on high government guaranteed prices are ultimately politically untenable because they are hugely expensive, unresponsive to the needs of customers and producers, insensitive to environmental and agronomic realities, and a shameful waste of economic assets. Rather than farming government programmes, our producers are looking for customers around the world.

While agricultural trade benefits consumers and producers alike, it is an area in which progressive reform is ardently opposed by entrenched domestic interests. Producers in some countries, cosseted by high guaranteed prices and protective tariffs, oppose any move toward greater market orientation. Intervention in the agricultural economy—measured by the Organisation for Economic Cooperation and Development by summing price supports, direct payments, and other support as a per cent of total agricultural production—has actually increased in some countries from the levels at the beginning of the Uruguay Round. In the last set of multilateral trade negotiations, countries began the process of dismantling protection and delinking farm support from production decisions. Consequently, reforms have been undertaken by some countries.

The WTO Opportunity

The major objective in the upcoming farm talks is to accelerate the reform process initiated in the Uruguay Round. That means further substantial negotiations on tariffs, subsidies, and other trade-distorting measures so that the level and other trade-distorting measures so that the level and direction of trade are determined by market forces, not government intervention. Four key areas are outlined below:

(i) **Export Competition:** Export subsidies are the most distorting trade tool because the level and direction of trade is directly determined by government subsidies. Today, the European Union (EU) is the only substantial export subsidizer—nearly all other countries agreed not to use, or have only limited resource to use, export subsidies in the last round of negotiations. EU farmers, responding to domestic prices frequently twice the world price, produce more products than can be consumed in Europe, but at such high prices that they can be sold abroad only with generous subsidies. These subsidies push other competitive supplies out of the market (which is expensive and unfair) and discourage production in countries that have a comparative advantage in agricultural production (which is wasteful and is threatening both to the environment and to future farm production needs).

In the Uruguay Round negotiations, countries acknowledged the corrosive nature of subsidies and agreed to cap and reduce their use. The upcoming negotiations should eliminate them to ensure that countries do not resort to other policy tools that allow government spending to determine winners in the marketplace. Specifically, WTO members should look closely at curbing distorting state trading agricultural export monopolies that can disguise subsidies and exert distorting market power, along with other policies used to dispose of surplus commodities on a nonmarket basis.

(ii) Market access: Measure applied at the border to stop trade currently are the principal barrier to a freer and more open trading environment for agriculture. Market access barriers deny efficient producers the chance to compete in other markets and limit the variety and quality of products available to consumers. Opening markets and maximizing trade opportunities as fundamental principles of WTO, and we still have a long way to go in agriculture to open markets to competition.

The Uruguay Round Agreement set agricultural trade on a more predictable basis by requiring that all non-tariff measures, such as quotas and import bans, be converted to simple tariffs. While this was a necessary first step to removing trade barriers, many of the tariffs are still prohibitively high. For example, while the average tariff assessed by the United States on agricultural products is less than 5 per cent (and nearly zero for industrial products), the average agriculture tariff-rate quota (TRQ). Where only specific quantities of imports receive low duties. Many other commodities also; are subject to high tariffs.

As we start the next century, higher tariffs should not stop the flow of imported agricultural products. Where TRQs remain as a transitional step before we achieve more open trade, we expect more specific disciplines on the way in which they are administered. Similarly, we need to take a hard look at agricultural state trading monopoly. Importers; use of these state traders may have been justifiable when more restrictions allowed on farm trade, but in the tariff-only regime it is hard to see why a government needs to insert itself between an exports and an end-user.

(iii) Domestic Subsidies: Domestic subsidy programmes are often the root cause of other-distorting polices. Subsidy policies that increase domestic prices above world price levels can be maintained only if price-competitive imports are restricted. Additionally, overproduction generated by high domestic prices can be sold on world markets only with export subsidies that bring the price down to the world price. While reining in distortive domestic subsidy programmes has value in its own right for rationalizing agricultural production, the WTO negotiations will focus on their trade-distorting elements.

In the Uruguay Round negotiations, countries, agreed to distinguish trade-distorting subsidies (generally those linked to the production of a specific crop or related to price supports) from non-trade distorting subsidies (such as research and development, training and environmental production). The trade-distorting subsidies were capped, and the process of reducing allowable levels of subsidies began. This distinction is a good one: the nasty sort of subsidy that distorts markets and straitjackets producers should be cut, while programmes that will increase a country's ability to produce agricultural products in the next century without distorting production incentives should not be reduced.

(iv) **Standards:** As WTO members make progress on cutting tariffs and subsidies, the temptation increase to disguise trade barriers as health and safety measures or other innocuous-sounding "technical standards". Moreover, when regulations purportedly designed to protected heath are instead vehicles for domestic protectionism, the credibility of the entire safety apparatus of a country is put up for questioning. When good science is replaced by politics, the basis for sound health policy is undermined. Therefore, increasing government accountability by putting the emphasis on sound science for health standards should discipline disguised barriers to trade and strengthen health policy.

In the Uruguay Round, countries agreed to a set of sound principles: each has the right to maintain health and safety measures, but these must be based on sound science, backed by scientific evidence and an assessment of the risk, and be no more trade-restrictive than required to meet health goals. In practice, countries have found that these principles work well—bogus measures adopted without scientific basis have been successfully challenged in the WTO without sacrificing health concerns. Creating a supportive environment for the propagation of yield-enhancing biotech products also is critical for meeting the needs of the coming century.

Agriculture is Different

Agriculture occupies a special place in the national economies of most countries around the world. Farmers are responsible for feeding and clothing people. Farming also holds a powerful claim on our national cultures that calls for the preservation of rural lifestyles and values. Farm production is subject to the cruel vagaries of whether and the relentless decline in prices and increases in costs. Some people point to these factors as justifying a different treatment for agriculture in the international economy, including justifying trade-distorting agricultural policies. This is wrong-headed; societies can support farms and preserve rural communities in ways that foster choice, protect natural resources, and expand trade.

Farm production in the next century cannot afford to be trapped in a static system in which prices are determined by government mandate, production decisions are controlled by central planners, and farmers are forced to produce only for local consumers. This myopic system cannot be sustained in any important agriculture producing society. Moreover, this type of system will not meet the needs of the coming century, when we will face unprecedented consumer demand and natural resource constraints.

Instead, I look forward to dynamic world of agricultural trade in which producers, exporters, and retailers apply the creativity of the human mind to the natural bounty of the earth. In this "new" world, we will produce a greater amount and variety of food than ever before, feed the coming billions, sustain our environment, and unlock economic resources otherwise stiffed by moribund protectionism, ultimately raising living standards around the world.

3

The Uruguay Round and Agricultural Reform

The Uruguay Round of Multilateral Trade Negotiations (completed in 1994) continued the process of reducing trade barriers achieved in seven previous rounds of negotiations. Among the Uruguay Round's most significant accomplishments were the adoption of new rules governing agricultural trade policy, the establishment of disciplines on the use of Sanitary and Phytosanitary (SPS) measures, and agreement on a new process for setting trade disputes. The Uruguay Round also created the World Trade Organisation (WTO) to replace the General Agreement on Tariffs and Trade (GATT) as an institutional framework for overseeing trade negotiations and adjudicating trade disputes. Agricultural trade concerns that have come to the fore since the Uruguay Round, including the use of genetically engineered products in agricultural trade, state trading, and a large number of potential new members, illustrate the wide range of issues any new round may face.

During the past years since initial implementation of the Uruguay Round agreements, the record with respect to agriculture is mixed. The Uruguay Round's overall impact on agricultural trade can be considered positive in moving toward several key goals, including reducing agricultural export subsidies, establishing new rules for agricultural import policy, and agreeing on disciplines for Sanitary and Phytosanitary trade measures. The Uruguay Round Agreement on Agriculture (URAA) may also have contributed to a shift in domestic support of agriculture away from those practices with the largest potential to affect production and, therefore, to affect trade flows. However, significant reductions in most agricultural tariffs will have to await a future round of negotiations.

Tariffs, Incentives, and Subsidies

Prior to Uruguay Round, trade in many agricultural products was unaffected by the tariff cuts that were made for industrial products in previous rounds. In the Uruguay Round, participating countries agreed to convert all nontariff agricultural trade barriers to tariffs (a process called "tarification") and to reduce them. However, agricultural tariffs remain very high for some products in some countries, limiting the trade benefits to be derived from the new rules. To ensure that historical trade levels were maintained and to create some new trade opportunities where trade had been largely precluded by policies, countries instituted tariff-rate quotas. A tariff-rate quota applies a lower tariff to imports below a certain quantitative limit (quota) and permits a higher tariff on imported goods after the quota has been reached.

The Agreement on Agriculture required countries to reduce outlays on domestic polices that provide direct economic incentives to producers to increase resources use or production. All WTO member countries are meeting their commitments to reduce these outlays, and most countries reduced this type of support. By more than the required amount. However, support from those domestic policies considered to have the least effect on production, such as domestic food aid, has increased from 1986-88 levels.

In the Agreement on Agriculture, 25 countries that employed export subsidies agreed to reduce the volume and value of their subsidized exports over a specified implementation period. To date, most of these countries have met their commitments, although some have found ways to circumvent them. The European Union (EU) is by far the largest user of export subsidies, according for 84 per cent of subsidy outlays of the 25 countries in 1995 and 1996. Despite substantial progress in reducing export subsidies, rising world grain supplies and falling world grain prices will make it difficult for some countries to meet future commitments unless they adopt policy changes.

The Uruguay Round's SPS agreement imposed disciplines on the use of measures to protect human, animal, and plant life and health from foreign pests, diseases, and contaminants. The agreement can be credited with increasing the transparency of countries SPS regulations and providing improved means for selling SPS-related trade disputes, including some important cases involving agricultural products. The agreement has also spurred regulatory reforms in some countries. The SPS agreement and the Agreement on Technical Barriers to Trade could provide a framework for disputes over Generally Modified Organisms (GMOs) brought to the WTO for arbitration.

Current Issues

Changes made to the multilateral dispute resolution process in the Uruguay Round may be as important to agricultural trade as the improvement in the substantive rules governing trade in agricultural goods. Initial evidence indicates that the WTO dispute settlement system is a significant improvement over its GATT predecessor. For example, a single country can no longer block the formation of a dispute resolution panel or veto an adverse ruling by blocking the adoption of a panel report. These improvements have led to a number of important agricultural trade cases being adjudicated before the WTO. The outstanding question for the WTO is whether members whose practices have been successfully challenged under the new dispute settlement procedures will live up to their obligations.

Other agriculture-related issues, including a bid for membership by a large and diverse group of potential new WTO members, the challenge of dealing with State Trading Enterprises (STEs) within WTO disciplines, and issues particular to developing countries, will shape the agenda for future agricultural trade liberalisation discussions. Thirty countries are currently seeking membership in the 134-member WTO. Countries seeking WTO membership accede under conditions negotiated with WTO membership through the privileged trade status with WTO member but may incur adjustment costs in reforming their trade policies and reducing tariffs to meet WTO requirements. Current WTO members gain greater access to the markets of acceding countries.

State trading enterprises, governmental and non-governmental entities that have been granted special rights or privileges through which they can influence trade, countries to be important to the trade of agricultural commodities because many countries consider them to be an appropriate means to meet domestic agricultural policy objectives. Continuing concerns about the trade practices of state trading enterprises in some WTO member countries and the potential accession of China and other countries where STEs are prominent will keep STEs on the WTO agenda.

Developing countries received special treatment in the Uruguay Round, including less stringent disciplines in reforming their trade policies than those apply to developed countries. In the next round of multilateral agricultural trade negotiations, developing countries will continue to have their own interests in the areas of special and differential treatment, export restraints, price stability, food security, food aid, and stock policies. As developing countries identify their positions, coalitions of countries with common trade interests may emerge.

4

WTO Agricultural Negotiations: *Completing the Task*

The Cairns Group of 15 agricultural-exporting countries was formed in 1986 to influence agricultural negotiations within the World Trade Organisation (WTO). It was largely as a result of the group's efforts that a framework for reform in farm products trade was established in the Uruguay Round and agriculture was for the first time subject to global trade liberalizing rules. The group is positioning itself to play an important role in the new round of WTO agricultural negotiations.

The Cairns Group, which accounts for about 20 per cent of world agricultural exports, includes both developed and developing countries across a diverse set of regions around the world. The group consists of Argentina, Australia, Brazil, Canada, Chile, Colombia, Fiji, Indonesia, Malaysia, New Zealand, Paraguay, Philippines, South Africa, Thailand, and Uruguay. By acting collectively, this disparate group has had more influence and impact on the agriculture negotiations than individual members would have had independently. Under Australian leadership, the group takes a consensual approach to decision-making.

Beyond the Uruguay Round

Members of the Cairns Group were generally pleased with the Uruguay Round outcome, but believe much remains to be done to ensure that a genuine market-oriented approach to agricultural policies is achieved. For example, in 1997 levels of agricultural support in Organisation for Economic Cooperation and Development (OECD) countries alone were still extremely high at $280 billion. The approach taken by the group to the challenge of reducing this assistance and creating a freer agricultural marketplace has been in two parts. First, the group has worked to ensure that countries meet the commitments that were agreed to in the agricultural-related agreements during the Uruguay Round. It has done this by remaining visible and active since the end of the round.

Second, the Cairns Group has been effective in engaging other WTO member countries in early preparation for the next round of agricultural negotiations in an attempt to ensure that they start on time and are not unnecessarily protracted as they were during the Uruguay Round. The Cairns Group in April 1998 agreed on a strongly worded "vision statement" conveying the Group's ambition and broad objectives for the 1999 agriculture negotiations and initiated a strategic approach to the preparations for the negotiations. This approach is necessarily ambitious. "The Cairns Group of Agricultural Fair Traders reaffirms its commitment to achieving a fair and market-oriented agricultural trading system as sought by the Agreement on Agriculture. To this end, the Caims Group is united in its resolve to ensure that the next WTO agriculture negotiations achieve fundamental reform which will put trade in agricultural goods on the same basis as trade in other goods. All trade-distorting subsidies must be eliminated and market access must be substantially improved so that agricultural trade can proceed on the basis of market forces."

Objectives for Negotiations

The vision statement outlines the Cairns Group's reform goals in three key areas within the Uruguay Round framework, as follows:

- Deep cuts to all tariffs are required, as well as the removal of tariff speaks and the redressing of tariff escalation so that market access for agricultural commodities and value-added agricultural products is on a similar footing as trade in other commercially traded products. This should include the objective of transforming market access barriers to tariffs and removal of nontariff barriers to trade. In the interim, the Caims Group supports substantial increases in trade volumes under tariff-rate quotas, while the administration of tariff-rate quotas must not diminish the size and value of market access opportunities, particularly in products of special interest to developing countries.

- All trade-distorting domestic supports must be eliminated or replaced with non-trade distorting methods of assistance. Income aids or other domestic support measures should be targeted, transparent, and fully decoupled so that they do not distort production and trade.
- Export subsidies must be made illegal for agricultural products, as they are for other traded goods, and clear rules must be established to prevent circumvention of export subsidy commitments. In this regard, it is worth nothing that only 25 of the 134 current WTO members are entitled to use export subsidies, and most of these are developed countries (with more than 80 per cent of export subsidies accounted for by the European Union). Also, agricultural export credits must be brought under effective international discipline with a view to ending government subsidisation of such credits.

Special Needs of Developing Countries

The vision statement also reaffirms the group's support for the principle of special and differential treatment for developing countries, including least-developed countries and small states, remaining an integral part of the next WTO agriculture negotiations. The Cairns Group ministers agreed that the framework for liberalisation must continue to support the economic development needs, including technical assistance requirements, of these WTO members. As has been stated by the Cairns Group: Major challenges facing many developing countries are the persistence of rural poverty and the linkages between such poverty and serious environmental problems. Consequently, more sustainable agricultural development remains a central policy issue in many developing countries. An improved international trading environment that is more conductive to supporting agricultural development is needed as an essential ingredient in addressing these problems.

Adherence to these principles will not only improve the trading environment for agricultural exporting nations, but will also have important implications for global food security. Food security will be enhanced through more diversified and reliable sources of supply, as more farmers, including poorer farmers in developing countries, are able to respond to market forces and new income-generating opportunities, without the burden of competition from heavily subsidized products. To provide further assurance to net-food-importing countries, export restrictions must not be allowed to disrupt the supply of food to world markets.

Reductions in assistance to the agricultural sector may also have positive implications for the environment. In many cases, agricultural subsidies and access restrictions have stimulated farm practices that are harmful to the environment. Reform of these policies can contribute to the development of environmentally sustainable agriculture.

Preparations for the Next Round

Cairns Group ministers welcomed the launch by the second WTO Ministerial Conference in Geneva in May 1998 of preparations for the next round of agriculture negotiations. The WTO Ministerial Declaration that emanated from this conference binds WTO members to a preparatory process that began in September 1998 and will culminate in ministerial agreement on a decision on the scope, structure, and time-frame for the agriculture negotiations.

The Cairns Group reaffirms its commitment to achieving a fair and market-oriented agricultural trading system as sought by the Agreement on Agriculture. To this end, the

Cairns Group is united in its resolve to ensure that the next WTO agriculture negotiations achieve fundamental reform that will place trade in agricultural goods on the same basis as trade in other goods.

5

Export Subsidies: *A Distortion to Free Trade in Agriculture*

Export subsidies are generally considered one of the most distorting trade tools used by governments to interfere with commercial markets. Export subsidies allow a government to determine the level and direction of trade solely on the basis of government subsidies, lowering world prices and denying sales for other, more competitive exporters. Not only are export subsidies unfair commercial tools, but, by encouraging surplus production, they encourage adverse environmental practices, waste government budgets, and may delay restructuring and reform of domestic industries. Substantial progress toward eliminating export subsidies will be a critical element of the World Trade Organisation (WTO) negotiations scheduled to begin at the end of this year.

The Situation Today

Under the Uruguay Round Agreement, countries agreed to strictly limit the use of export subsidies. First, products that had not benefited from export subsidies in the past were banned from receiving them in the future. Second, where countries had provided export subsidies in the past, their future use was capped and gradually reduced over 6 to 10 years. (Developed countries were required to cut their spending on export subsidies by 36 per cent over six years while also reducing subsidized export quantities by at least 21 per cent on a commodity-specific basis.

Developing countries have until 2005 to cut spending by 24 per cent and subsidized quantities by 14 per cent). Third, countries agreed not to create new schemes that serve as disguised subsidies to get around the product-specific limits. Finally, countries recognized that export credit and food aid programmes were different and exempted them from the new budget and quantity limits, although there was agreement to negotiate disciplines on export credit programmes to ensure that they do not undermine WTO commitments.

Today, the European Union (EU) is the primary export subsidizer—accounting for nearly 85 per cent of the world total. Nearly all other countries agreed in the last round of negotiations not to use or to have only limited recourse to use export subsidies. EU farmers, responding to domestic prices that are often twice the world price, produce more products than can be consumed in Europe, but at such high prices that they can be sold abroad only with generous subsidies. These subsidies force other competitors out of the market and discourage production in countries with comparative advantage.

If the EU's extravagant domestic subsidies are the root cause of export subsidies, they are also putting serious pressure on the whole EU system. The need to impose budgetary discipline on EU farm programmes (annual cost, about $48 billion is becoming increasingly evident, even in Europe, and the EU's goal of expanding its membership to new countries is putting pressure on it to bring its farm programmes into line with other countries, which will help reduce its need to rely on export subsidies in the future.

Areas for Resolution

The upcoming negotiations should continue the work begun in the Urguay Round and eliminate existing export subsidies. There is no economic justification for their continued use. By removing subsidized exports, world prices should increase, and farmers, particularly in the EU, will not be artificially encouraged to overproduce products that they cannot grow competitively.

In addition to eliminating export subsidies, countries should examine the rules defining export subsidies to ensure that countries do not resort to other policy tools that might allow governments to distort markets. Specially, WTO members should to look closely at curbing agricultural state trading export monopolies that can exert undue market power or dispose of surplus commodies on a nonmarket basis. A recent WTO victory by the United States and New Zealand over Canada's special-class system of dairy exports shows that the existing rule against circumvention are effective but must be enforced.

Export credit and food aid programmes were addressed in the Uruguay Round agreement in recognition of the fact that those tools could be disguised as subsidies. These policies may again be on the agenda when the WTO negotiations commence next time. It will be important to ensure that the world's needy continue to have access to imported products, even when financial turmoil roils would markets and limits the ability of developing countries to meet their food and fiber needs.

Certain large exporting nations—primarily in the EU have used export taxes as a supply management tool by intervening in the market to restrict exports when domestic stocks are low. These measures can wreak havoc in international markets, exacerbating price swings and reducing the confidence of net-food-importing countries to abandon trade barriers and rely on the international market to provide food security. Similarly, some exporting countries use differential export taxes to discourage exports of basic products (such as grains or oilseeds); they force exporters to process the product domestically (into four or oil and meal, for example) and export the value added products.

6

Developing Countries and the WTO Agricultural Negotiations

Developing countries as a group have much to gain from continued progress toward a transparent, rule-based trading system in agriculture. The researches say the negotiations should eliminate export subsidies, impose stricter disciplines on export taxes, cut tariffs, and ensure that food aid continues to be available to poor countries in grant form and delivered so as not to displace domestic production in the countries receiving it. Badly managed food aid, or cheap food imports due to export subsidies, may just reinforce the bias of economic policies against the rural sector. With its negative impact on poor agricultural producers, "they say. International research organisations (such as IFPRI, among other institutions) may provide support to developing countries through programmes of collaborative research, technical assistance, and capacity strengthening.

Starting with the first round of trade negotiations under the General Agreement on Tariffs and Trade (GATT) after World War II, there has been a relatively steady trend of increasing multilateral trade liberalisation. The successive rounds of negotiations recognized the greater needs of developing countries, especially since the Tokyo Round. Yet the participation of developing countries was limited. Since many developing countries were not members of GATT, the major forum for airing their views was provided by the United Nations Conference on Trade and Development. The views of developing countries had some impact on the Lome agreements and on aid flows, but had limited influence on negotiations concerning trading rules, which were discussed within the frame work of the GATT, where OECD (Organisation for Economic Cooperation and Development) countries set the agenda.

In the Uruguay Round, which began in 1986 and concluded in 1993, developing countries played a larger role in the negotiations compared to previous rounds. In particular, agricultural net exporters organized the Cairns Group (which in addition to Australia, New Zealand, and Canada, included several large developing countries such as Argentina, Brazil, Indonesia, and the Philippines) to pursue their interests. Furthermore, during and after the conclusion of the Uruguay Round, the formal accession of developing countries to the GATT and now the World Trade Organisation (WTO) has continued apace. Of the 134 members of the WTO in February 1999, some 70 per cent were developing countries. The United Nations classified 48 countries as least-developed (LLDCs). Within that group, 29 are members of the WTO, six are in the process of accession, and three are observers. Also, 18 countries have been identified as net-food-importing developing countries (NFIDCs).

Some Definitions

The LLDCs are identified by the United Nations General Assembly based on several criteria—income per capita, augmented physical quality of life index, and an index of economic diversification. As a group, they have a population of about 590 million people, with an income per capita about 4 per cent that of the world average (1996). Agricultural production per capita in LLDCs has been declining since the 1970s although the same indicator for all developing countries (mainly under the influence of China) has gone up by nearly 40 per cent in the same period. LLDCs represent a small fraction of world trade (less than 1 per cent for total and about 2 per cent for agricultural trade). They had a positive, although declining net agricultural trade balance until the mid 1980s, when it turned negative. Almost 20 per cent of their total imports are food items.

The 18 net-food-importing developing countries have been selected through a process within the WTO. They have a population of some 380 million people and an income per capita nearly five times that of the LLDC average, but still much lower than the world average. NFIDCs are a diverse group: four are upper-middle income countries; eight are lower-middle income; and six are lower income. Four of them had net food exports on average during 1995-97, but because they imported cereals they are included in the group. NFIDCs, per capita food production as share of both world and developing country averages has risen, although from very low levels.

Although the categories of "developed" and "developing" countries have important legal consequences under WTO rules, there are no formal definitions of either category. The process works through self-identification and negotiation with other member countries of the WTO.

Completing the Unfinished Agenda

In general, developing countries operate under what has been called "special and differential treatment". They face lower disciplines and enjoy longer time frames for implementing reforms. In the case of LLDCs, they are totally exempt from WTO commitments, and it has been agreed that developing and least-developed countries should receive special consideration for market access and technical and financial support. Also, during the Uruguay Round, concerns that liberalisation of agricultural policies and trade could adversely affect the food imports of LLDCs and NFIDCs led participants to include several measures dealing with food security issues in the "green box" of permitted domestic support—for instance, the formation of public stockholding and the provision of foodstuffs at subsidized prices. These was a ministerial decision in Marrakesh in April 1994 to deal with possible negative effects of agricultural trade reforms on the food security of LLDCs and NFIDCs. The decision was reemphasized at the 1996 ministerial meeting of the WTO in Singapore.

Export and Domestic Subsidies: While many developing countries have significantly reduced distorting domestic agricultural policies, the possible benefits that these countries and the world an enjoy are thwarted by the subsidies of developed countries. The Uruguay Round was a first step in imposing discipline on the unfair competition arising from subsidized agricultural exports, which hurts poor agricultural producers in developing countries irrespective of their net agricultural trade position. In the next negotiations, that first step should be completed with the elimination of export subsidies. Net-food-importing developing countries should also be interested in stricter disciplines on export taxes and controls that exacerbate price fluctuations in world markets.

Under the Uruguay Round agreement, there is still a lot of scope for the developed countries to use domestic subsidies, in addition to the use of export subsidies; to help their farmers. The developing countries should seek further disciplines in this regard, including, among other things, the elimination of exemptions under the "blue box" (which allows farmers to receive some forms of direct payments that are considered to be trade distorting). Least-developed and developing countries, however, will still be allowed "special and differential treatment" on these issues.

Market Access: If the developing countries are to succeed in diversifying their agricultural sectors, they need expanded access to markets in developed countries.

This includes increasing the volume of imports allowed under the current regime of tarifffrate quotas (TRQs, which replaced the previous system of rigid quotas with a combination of a quantitative quota and a high tariff for the eventual out-of-quota imports); making the administration of the TRQs more transparent and equitable; seeking further reductions in tariffs, particularly those still high in some key products; and completing the process of tariffication in the cases where exemptions were granted. Also, eliminating, or at least reducing, tariff escalation in non-agricultural products is important for developing countries: this practice undermines the possibilities of expanding production and exports of processed goods that use agricultural inputs, exploiting "forward linkages" in the value-added chain.

What the Most Vulnerable Need

The special situation and concerns of least-developed countries and net-food-importing countries were recognized in a ministerial decision agreed upon at the completion of the Uruguay Round in 1993. These concerns include the preservation of adequate levels of food aid, the provision of technical assistance and financial support to develop the agricultural sector in those countries, and the continuation and expansion of financial facilities to help with structural; adjustment and short-term difficulties in financing food import. It is important to make food aid available in grant form, to target it to poor countries and social groups, and to deliver it in ways that do not displace domestic production in the countries receiving it. Bodly managed food aid, or cheap food imports due to export subsidies, may just reinforce the bias of economic policies against the rural sector, with its negative impact on poor agricultural producers.

Volatility in agricultural prices must be monitored carefully. While expansion of world agricultural trade should limit overall fluctuations by spreading supply and demand shocks over larger areas, the decline in world public stocks as a percentage of consumption works in the opposite direction. Improving early warning of potential food shortages, lowering costs for food transportation and storage, and providing better targeted food aid programmes and financial facilities for emergencies are also issues that need to be addressed by countries participating in thc coming round of negotiations.

The impact of changes in trade and agricultural policy on poorer consumers and producers in developing countries is a matter of debate. Some have argued that trade liberalisation may hurt both groups. Others have answered that greater productivity and growth coming from better trade and soctoral policies should help generate employment and income, given a setting of adequate overall economic policies and properly functioning markets and social institutions.

Small producers will also be helped by the disciplines that the URAA is bringing to subsidized and dumped exports, while it allows the implementation of a variety of programmes aimed at poor producers or consumers, including stocks for food security purposes and domestic food aid for populations in need. The issue here is the adequate design and funding of domestic policies to achieve the intended objectives of agricultural growth and poverty alleviation, which most certainly will not be helped by trade-distorting interventions either in developed or developing countries.

In general, low-income developing countries and LLDCs should emphasize to the international community the importance of creating and expanding a supportive international trade and financial environment and of implementing an integrated framework for economic and social development, with agricultural and trade policies being an integral part of the strategy. Appropriate measures would include—in addition to the agricultural trade issue suggested here—the continuation and enhancement of the reduction of the external debt of Heavily Indebted Poor Countries (the HIPC initiative and the further liberalisation of trade in textiles.

But improved international conditions should go hand-in-hand with a better domestic framework in developing and least-developed countries, including stable macro economic policies, open and effective markets, good governance, the rule of law, a vibrant civil society, and programmes and investments that expand opportunities for all, with special consideration for poor and disadvantaged groups.

Bringing Developing Countries into the Process

Developing countries, as small players in the global arena, should be interested and active participants in the design and implementation of international rules that limit the ability of larger countries to resort to unilateral action. Also, domestic legal and institutional frameworks in developing countries may be strengthened by the implementation of internationally negotiated rules that limit the scope for rent seeking and arbitrary projectionist measures. The developing countries as a group have much to gain from continued progress toward a transparent, rule-based, trading system in agriculture.

What are the requirements and skills for the developing countries to become effective members in the next WTO round? Any negotiation requires careful consideration of the legal, economic and political dimensions that define the substance and possible evolution of the negotiations, as well as the diplomatic and negotiating techniques that may help in the attainment of the expected outcomes. Questions that need to be addressed include:

- What are the economic and social consequences of different WTO scenarios (quantitative estimation of impacts)? Knowing the impacts of alternative scenarios is crucial if deveoing countries are to represent their interests in the negotiation process.
- What are the legal issues being discussed (definition of obligations, exemptions, time frame, and so on)? Detailed knowledge of international trade law is crucial if developing countries are not to be "short-changed." The devil is in the details.
- Looking at the political process, who are the main actors and their interests and what type of alliances may drive the negotiations? Negotiators must understand the political economy of their own country and of other countries in the WTO if they are to negotiate effectively.
- With these elements, an adequate diplomatic and negotiating strategy must be defined and implemented.

Developing countries that have carefully considered all four components will be better prepared to participate effectively in the coming negotiations. Of course, limited financial and human resources act as an important constraint. However, developing countries may overcome some of the problems through collective action, for instance considering the creation of alliances with respect to their main export and import commodities and the markets they approach for their exports. An example is the Cairns Group. This approach could reduce the fixed costs of negotiations., Spreading them over groups of countries, allow a better use of scarce technical expertise, and improve the bargaining position of developing countries. It could also be in the interest of the OECD countries to deal with negotiating blocs, which represent a smaller number of negotiating positions, rather than with numerous separate countries. The negotiations would be much more efficient and balanced.

7

The Uruguay Round Agreement on Agriculture

The Uruguay Round Agreement on Agriculture (URAA) calls for the initiation of negotiations for continuing the process of agricultural trade reform in 1999. Article 20 of the agreement states that member countries of the World Trade Organisation (WTO) recognize that the long-term objective of substantial progressive reductions in trade distorting support and protection of agriculture resulting in fundamental reforms is an ongoing process.

The Uruguay Round Agreement on Agriculture, which entered into force in 1995 along with other Uruguay Round accords, including the agreement to establish the World Trade Organisation, was an important step toward applying multilateral rules and disciplines to global agricultural trade. Most assessments of the agreement hail it as a historic shift in the way agriculture establishes new multilateral trade agreements. The agreement establishes new multilateral rules governing market access, export subsidies and domestic support for agriculture. In terms of future trade liberalisation, its most important provisions may be those requiring the elimination of quantitative trade restrictions and their conversion to bound tariffs. These bound tariffs, even if some of them are extremely high, can provide a starting point for future negotiations of tariff reductions.

Market Access

The agreement requires all WTO members to convert

nontariff trade barriers to tariffs and to reduce them by a simple average of 36 per cent over six years (with a minimum tariff reduction per tariff line of 15 per cent). The agreement prohibits the introduction of new nontariff barriers to trade. Where nontariffs barriers restrict imports, the agreement requires that importing countries offer minimum access of usually 3 per cent of consumption rising to 5 per cent over the six-year implementation period for the agreement.

Most assessments of the agreement conclude that it provides little in the way of expanded access for agricultural products. Its importance lies in extending the principle (already applied to trade in industrial products) of protection by bound tariffs to agricultural trade and establishing at least a base for further tariffs reductions in future negotiations.

Export Subsidies

The agreement requires that export subsidies be reduced by 21 per cent in terms of quantities and by 36 per cent in terms of budgetary outlays by the end of the six-year implementation period. WTO members may continue to use their existing export subsidies within the limits established, but may not introduce any new export subsidies.

Domestic Support

The agreement also includes rules and commitments for domestic support. Domestic subsidies are to be cut by 20 per cent from average levels of support aggregated across all commodities for the base period 1986-88. Support reduction commitments are also to be made over the six-year implementation period on the basis of this aggregate measure of support (AMS).

Trade policy experts contend that the rules established for domestic support policies are more important than the reduction commitments required. The agreement defines which domestic policies are permitted ("green box" policies), such as income support provided to farmers independently of participation in production-limiting programmes, advisory services, or domestic food assistance. Policies that are not eligible for the green box are automatically prohibited ("amber box" policies.)

Sanitary and Phytosanitary Measures

An agreement on the Application of Sanitary and Phytosanitary (SPS) Measures reaffirms the right of WTO members to adopt and enforce measures that they deem appropriate to protect human, animal, or plant life or health as long as such measures are not applied in an "arbitrary and unjustified" manner. The agreement states that such measures may not be used as disguised barriers to trade. SPS measures may be based on international standards where they exist. WTO members could impose higher standards than those derived from these sources if based on scientific justification and risk assessment. All WTO members agree to recognise the equivalence of different standards that result in a comparable level of SPS protection. Dispute settlement panels should seek advice from relevant international organisations when scientific or technical matters are at issue.

The SPS Agreement, though binding on WTO members, is stated in broad language. Specific will come from interpretation of the agreement and adjudication of sanitary and Phytosantitary issues in WTO dispute settlement.

Dispute Settlement

New and strengthened dispute settlement procedures agreed to as pat of the Uruguay Round also apply to disputes that may arise under either the Agreement on Agriculture or the SPS Agreement. An important change in WTO dispute settlement procedures is the elimination of a member's right to veto a dispute Panel's decision and effectively block implementation of the Panel's recommendations for resolving the dispute. Potentially this strengthens the ability of the WTO to enforce panel judgements. The right of WTO members to negotiate compensation rather than change its challenged policies remains in place, however.

8

Food First

By the time this day is over, about 40,000 human beings—mostly children—will have died from hunger, malnutrition and related causes. Today and every day the deaths will mount, reaching an annual toll of 13 to 18 million. Few of these people will have been caught up in famine or other emergencies. Most will have suffered from a "silent" assault—the kind that seldom makes the headlines, but which claims its victims just as relentlessly.

It is intolerable that such deprivation and suffering should be allowed to exist in a world of potential food plenty. Having enough food is fundamental to all else. At the most basic level, this may entail humanitarian relief to assist people in emergency situations. In the transition from relief to development, however, we must look at systems for ensuring that societies have the capacity to produce or purchase the food they need and that it is accessible to all.

Sustainable food security fuses the goals of household food security and sustainable agriculture; it requires both. It requires looking not only at the aggregate supply of food, but also at the distribution of income and land, and at other issues: Do people have enough income to buy food? Enough land to grow their own food? Does the food distribution system deliver food where it is needed? How much food is wasted due to inadequate distribution systems? What are the implications of trends in population growth for future food needs? What is the status of women in society, and what opportunities do women have to alter rapid population growth rates? What is being done to regenerate the resource base for food production? These questions need to be asked and answered in every country.

The challenge of sustainable food security is immense, and it is growing. One billion people—20 per cent of the global population—are too poor to obtain enough food to sustain normal work. Half a billion are too poor to obtain the food needed for healthy growth of children and minimal activity of adults. Today's failure to feed people, however, may be but a prologue to a much larger failure in the future. Given likely population increases, world food output must triple over the next 50 years if the world's people are to have a nutritionally adequate diet. It will be difficult enough to achieve this expansion under favourable circumstances, and conditions may be far from favourable.

For example, according to recent estimates an area of about 1.2 billion hectares—the size of China and India combined—has experienced moderate to extreme soil deterioration since World War II as a result of human activities. Over three-fourths of that deterioration has occurred in the developing regions from causes much as overgrazing, deforestation, land clearing, unsound agricultural practices and increased soil salinity and water logging, largely from irrigation. Other environmental threats to the agricultural resource base include loss of water and genetic resources, adverse effects of pesticides and climate change, both local and global.

At the most aggregate level, the required increase in food production could be met if production grew at the historic average, that is, at the two per cent per annum rate achieved over the past half-century. But is this realistic? To produce three times more calories, all the land currently under cultivation around the world ,within 50 years, have to attain levels of productivity as high as those exhibited by the very best cropland today.

To this challenge add the possibility of diminished returns from the technological, energy and other inputs that have made agriculture so successful. Some experts believe that most of the potential for increased output of cereals—from improved plant varieties, from increased use of pesticides and fertilizers and from expanding the area under irrigation—has already been captured.

Viewed from this perspective, the goal of achieving sustainable food security in the decades ahead emerges as one of the greatest challenges humanity has ever faced. Agricultural output must be tripled, and people must have the income to buy the food they need. The erosion of the resource base must be halted and then reversed. Failure on any of these fronts will yield unprecedented human suffering.

What will it take to achieve sustainable food security? Obviously, the effort will have to be immense, both in size and complexity. Outlined below are a few simple (but no easy) steps that are absolutely essential elements of serious effort.

First, as citizens of the world, we must all come to see sustainable food security as a fundamental aspect of global peace and human security. This goes well beyond merely denouncing the use of food as a weapon.

Second, we must adopt concrete international goals, such as reducing world hunger by half over the next 10 years. We will never achieve the goal of sustainable food security unless we aim at specific milestones, and assess rigorously our progress in moving toward them.

Third, we must forge a true global partnership, a compact for sustainable food security. All countries—rich and poor—have important roles and responsibilities. There must be reciprocal responsibilities among nations, not one-way transfers.

Fourth, we must see deterioration of the agricultural resource base—terrestrial, aquatic and climatic—for what it is: a major threat to development and a major source of economic loss. Farmers are the largest group of environmental decision-makers in the world. We must ensure that they have the means to make sustainable development a reality where it counts—in the fields and fisheries.

Fifth, we must empower the people who work the land and who keep it productive. They are in the best position to decide the most appropriate ways to graft new technology onto their own traditional knowledge of seed selection, plant protection and nutrient-cycling. Special emphasis should be given to the role of women, the main providers for two-thirds of the poorest housholds in the developing world, as well as the producers of 60 per cent of all food grown and consumed locally.

Sixth, we must build the capacities of developing countries, both in government and in civil society. Capacity-building means empowerment for self-reliance. It means strengthening national capacities, both inside and outside government. This is essential for recognition and analysis of problems, for decision-making on courses of action and for management of systems and processes.

Seventh, not only must we build capacity in developing countries, we must also create linkages among researchers in industrial and developing countries. This will help minimize the time lag between discovered and practical utilisation. In addition, analysts from various countries must work together to examine future food security issues with different scenarios of population growth, agricultural productivity, markets and trade, climate change, loss of soil and bio-diversity and, last but not least, political instability, in order to devise options for rational choices.

We know a good deal about how to rid the world of the scourge of hunger, and how to begin to move toward sustainable food security on a global basis. We know that economic growth and prosperity are necessary, though not sufficient conditions for eradicating hunger. We also know that development efforts must encompass not only food production, but also socio-economic factors, including sustainable livelihoods for poor families, the implications of population growth rates, the status of women and girls and so fourth. We also know that good words are not enough. Now more than ever before it is crucial that we marshal the political will to achieve our goals.

9

India's Food Challenge

Is India's population growing disproportionately to its food supply? Will famine once again hit millions of people? Most agriculture experts agree that a Malthusian crisis is not likely to occur in the near term. The reason; the overall food situation in India has been characterized by a large increase in regional output since the famine-ravaged 1960s.

At that time, the food situation was described as "desperate" in India. Famine had plagued India's Bihar state in the sixties. International food specialists predicted further famine because food production looked as if it would lag for behind population growth. Instead, average crop yields per acre soared, thanks to the introduction of high-yielding varieties of rice and wheat and to expanded irrigation and chemical fertilizer use. It has been called the "Green Revolution".

Double Role of Irrigation

The keys to the higher food production have been irrigation, the adoption of high-yielding varieties (HYVs) of foodgrains and the increased use of modern inputs such as fertilizers. Irrigation has played a double role, it has not only helped raise yields through synergistic interaction with HYVs and fertilizers, but has also contributed to considerable increases in harvested area by enabling higher cropping intensity.

Still, there are ominous clouds on Indian food horizon. In light of the region's high population growth, increased urban sprawl and rampant environmental degradation, there are signs that hunger problems could loom unless action is taken by Indian's and international development agencies.

Shrinking Base

The favourable food supply situation is likely to disappear within the next decade, due to a shrinking resource base, The earlier decades had witnessed a natural resource based growth strategy as there was adequate land and water resources for development. But this is fast disappearing due to urbanisation, industrialisation and ecological degradation. we should also remember that about 50 per cent of food production is from rainfed lands and a few years of drought couple alter the food security which we now enjoy. The high costs of irrigation and land development, could with low commodity prices, are also hampering required investments and these effects will be seen in the next decade.

"By the year 2030, India will have to produce 60 per cent more rice with much fewer resources. Clearly, there will be a major challenge for scientists and policy-makers to meet the increased food demand. India's population is growing 2 per cent a year, making the challenges for regional food security a daunting task.

The solution for meeting future food demand will be breakthroughs in science and technology since yield levels have reached a plateau and are even showing signs of decline. The possibilities through biotechnology and genetic engineering are exciting and can herald another "green revolution". This is the only hope for avoiding the Malthusian dilemma.

In gauging the region's population-food squeeze, it is useful to look first at its swelling population. India—the world's second populous region contains several states with high population growth rates.

Ironic Problem

Rapid population growth dilutes and impedes economic development. An increase in the population base puts greater pressure on finite resources, both financial and natural, and, in the context, worsening of income distribution, increased poverty incidence and environmental degradation.

Moreover, there is the ironic problem, that although rapid population growth increases poverty, poverty encourages larger families through its impact on access to education and decreased prospects for child survival.

If population growth is uncontrolled, the economic and social consequences are:

- ecological imbalance, with greater pressure on natural resources;
- increased urban crowding, with increases in demand for municipal services and infrastructure;
- a more unequal income distribution, particularly as labour supply outpaces job creation;
- signs of mass poverty, including high infant and child mortality rates, high levels of child malnutrition and hunger, poor school performance, unemployment and underemployment.

Bleak Prospects

Existing population growth rate is unsustainable, even for the relatively near future. Unless population growth rate is kept within manageable limits, the prospects for creating acceptable standards of living for low-income groups in India will be bleak.

The Indian population is growing more rapidly than ever before and will continue to do so for at least four decades. Indeed, without major technological breakthroughs and changes in patterns of consumption, even the most optimistic population growth projections are likely to be accompanied by increase in poverty, hunger and environmental degradation.

Whether we look at population, the environment or development, the next 10 years will be critical for our future, The decisions we make or don't take will widen or narrow our options for a century to come. They could decide the fate of the earth as a home for human beings.

10

Food Security: *Availability and Access to Food*

The world food situation has never been better. Enough food is being produced today that, if it were evenly distributed, no one should have to go hungry. World food production is increasing faster than population growth: per capital production increased by 5 per cent during the 1980s. Real food prices are at historic lows and have been declining for some time now. Yields of major cereals have more than doubled in the past three decades. These trends have contributed to complacency in some quarters regarding the world food situation.

Yet, more than 700 million people in the developing world do not have access to sufficient food to lead healthy and productive lives. More than 180 million children are underweight. Diseases of hunger and malnutrition are widespread. The desire to satisfy food needs has, in combination with increasing population densities and inadequate agricultural intensification, led to much degradation of environmentally fragile lands, such as foress and steep hillsides.

Over the next 20-30 years, farmers and policy makers in developing countries will be challenged to provide food at affordable prices for almost 100 million more people every year—the largest annual population increase in history. Moreover, they will have to increase food production from more productive use of the land and without further degradation of natural resources: area expansion is no longer a feasible option in most of the world.

What future food security will look like depends not on exogenous factors over which we have no control but on the decisions and actions taken by the major players: households, privates and public sector agencies, governments, and the international community. If we continue to act as we have in the 1980s and early 1990s, more people will suffer from food insecurity it will be because some or all of these players failed to at in an appropriate and timely manner.

Feeding the World: Availability and Access to Food

There is enough food in the world today to feed everyone, if it were evenly distributed. Availability of daily food energy per capita in the developing countries as a whole increased by 0.7 per cent per year during the 1980s.

Twenty-five developing countries, including about half of the African countries, were unable to assure sufficient food energy (2,200 calories per person per day) for their populations at the end of the 1980s even if available food energy were evenly distributed within each country. This is down from 45 countries at the end of the 1970s.

However, available food is neither evenly distributed nor fully consumed. Availability of enough food at global, regional, or national levels does not necessarily mean that everyone is well fed. For people to be food secure—that is, to have access at all times to the food required for a healthy and productive life—there must be both availability of food and access to food. Access to food by households (and individuals) is conditioned by poverty: the poor usually lack adequate means to secure access to food.

Over 1.1 billion people in developing countries were living in poverty in 1993, more than 500 million in conditions of extreme poverty. South Asia is the home of about 50 per cent of the developing world's poor—more than 500 million people. Another 15 per cent are found in East Asia, 19 per cent in sub-Saharan Africa, and 10 per cent in Latin America and the Caribbean. The prevalence of poverty (the proportion of each region's population that is poor) is very high—about 50 per cent—in South Asia as well as in sub-Saharan Africa.

Today, there are more than 700 million people who do not have access to sufficient food to meet their needs for a healthy and productive life; they often go hungry adults and children also suffer from diseases associated with hunger and poverty. For almost one fifth of the total population of developing countries to be chronically hungry tarnishes the images of a world that is now considered food-secure because it produces enough food.

Great progress has been made in meeting food needs during the last 30 years. For instance, the number of underfed people declined from an estimated 976 million in 1974-76 to 786 million in late 1980s. But the problem is far from solved. Keeping up with increasing needs and demands due to population growth, income increases, and dietary changes is itself a formidable challenge.

Hunger and food insecurity have a significant effect on health and nutrition of both adults and children. They can lead to growth failure in children. About 184 million pre-school children in developing countries were underweight in 1994. About 55 per cent of these underweight children were found in South Asia and another 16 per cent in sub-Saharan Africa. The proportion of children that are underweight is higher in South Asia (almost 60 per cent), but it is also significant in Sub-Saharan Africa (30 per cent) and Southeast Asia (31 per cent). It is worrisome that the number of underweight children in Sub-Saharan Africa during the 1980s from 20 million to 28 million is particularly striking.

In addition to energy deficiencies, micro nutrient deficiencies are also widespread in the developing world. About 14 million pre-school children (under the age of five years) have eye damage as a result of Vitamin-A deficiency. Ten million of these children are found in Southeast Asia. Between 250,000 and 500,000 pre-school children go blind each year due to Vitamin-A deficiency, two-thirds of these children die within months of going blind. Many more children are mildly affected. Recently research has shown that even mild deficiencies can increase mortality significantly. Vitamin-A deficiencies are closely linked to diet, which can be influenced by agricultural research and policy.

Iron deficiency affects about 1 billion people in the world. particularly children and women of reproductive age. Iron deficiency leads to anaemia, which if not checked can diminish learning capacity and increase morbidity and morality. In the developing countries, about 370 million women between 15 and 49 years of age—42 per cent of this population group—where anaemic in the 1980s. Almost one-half were in South Asia. And there are tentative indications from South Asia and sub-Saharan Africa that the prevalence of anaemia is rising in non pregnant adult women of reproductive ages.

In sub-Saharan Africa, this trend is undoubtedly associated with deterioration in general standards of living, including increased poverty and food insecurity. Anaemia partly arises from diets insufficient in iron, which again could be addressed through agricultural research and policy. For example, a possible reason why iron deficiency and anaemia are going up in South Asia may lie in the decrease in production of iron rich pulses during that same period, which in part reflects the larger research input into competing crops such as wheat in South Asia. This emphasizes the importance of considering the effects on diet and thus on health and nutrition in setting research priorities for yield-increasing research.

South Asia is the home of about half of the developing world's hungry and food-insecure people, but this population group is growing rapidly in sub-Saharan Africa. Much of the poverty and food insecurity is in rural areas, mainly in low-potential areas such as arid zones, but urban poverty is also growing rapidly.

Four Key Factors will Influence Future Food Production and Consumption

Global and regional food production and consumption during the next 10-20 years will be influenced by a large number of factors. Changes in the following four sets of factors are likely to particularly important:

1. Economic growth and economic policies;
2. Population growth and urbanisation;

3. Rural infrastructure, agricultural production technology, and access to modern inputs; and
4. Natural resource management and environmental consideration.

The expected impact of each of these factors on future food production and consumption is considerable.

Economic Growth and Economic Policies

Economic growth must resume in the developing world, especially in Sub-Saharan Africa. To support such growth, it is critical to:

- complete structural adjustment and economic reforms;
- remove external barriers to growth such as trade distortions and subsidies in developed countries;
- liberalize trade and remove market distortions;
- enhance access by the poor to land, capital, and technology;
- expand investment in rural infrastructure, health, education, and agricultural research and technology;
- facilitate sustain ability in agricultural production; and
- reverse the decline in international assistance to agriculture.

Growth in real per capita income during the 1980s was disappointing for developing countries as a whole. However, the low average rate of growth covers large variations among regions. The high rates of economic growth in Asia are expected to continue through the 1990s, while incomes in Sub-Saharan Africa are expected to keep pace with population growth.

Future economic growth depends on internal policies as well as on the international policies as well as on the international environment. The extent to which current structural adjustment and economic reforms in Latin America, Sub-Saharan Africa, the Commonwealth of Independent States (CIS), Eastern Europe, and selected countries in Asia and the Middle East are carried to successful completion at an appropriate speed and sequence is of paramount importance for future economic growth in those countries.

Closely related to this issue is the question of the most appropriate role of the stable in a market-oriented economy with inappropriate institutions, poor infrastructure, and insufficient experience by the private sector in dealing effectively in a competitive market environment. Overreaction to past failures such as excessive and inappropriate state intervention may cause governments to take on a passive role where intervention is needed to assure that the markets function effectively and to deal with outside influences on the economy.

Future economic growth will also depend on the international trade environment, including trade distortions by developed countries, and access to external aid. Import restrictions for agricultural and non-agricultural products in Japan, the European Union, and the United States, along with domestic agricultural subsidies and implicit and explicit export subsidies for agricultural products, are of particular concern.

Population Growth and Urbanisation

If progress in economic growth is not to be undermined by rapid population growth and excessive urbanisation, effective population and migration policies are necessary to complement growth-oriented policies. Such policies must focus on:

- universal access to family planning information and technology; and
- incentives to reduce rural-urban migration, such as provision of employment in rural areas and stimulation of agricultural and non-agricultural growth in rural areas.

Although the annual growth rate is falling for the world as a whole, the population increase during the next 20-30 years, of slightly less than 100 million people a year, will be the largest ever. Approximately 97 per cent of this increase is projected to occur in the Third World, with Africa alone accounting for 34 per cent of the growth. Thus although reductions in annual population growth rates have begun to occur in Asia and Latin America, they are insufficient to counter the absolute increases. Population growth rates of these magnitudes will greatly increase the need for food and other basic necessities.

Rural Infrastructure, Agricultural Production Technology, and Access to Modern Inputs

Continued progress in all three of these areas is critical to future food security.

- Resources must be committed to infrastructure construction and maintenance. Labour-intensive public works programmes are a viable mechanisms for building roads, reforesting areas, and engaging in soil conservation projects, while creating employment and income in rural areas.
- International and national agricultural research must continue to develop yield-enhancing production technology, especially in maize, millet, and other crops, as well as build tolerance or resistance in crops to pests and adverse climatic conditions.
- Farmer access to modern inputs must be facilitated through provision of credit and technical assistance. Inputs must be made available to all farmers on time and in required amounts.

The importance of investments in rural infrastructure within the context of rapid urbanisation has already been established. Even without rapid urban growth, however, such investments are needed in many developing countries, particularly the poorest ones, to facilitate agricultural and rural development. Improved rural infrastructure enhances access to export markets, modern production inputs, and consumer goods. It reduces marketing costs, promotes exchange between intracountry markets, reduces spatial and temporal price distortions, and, in general, increases efficiency in production and marketing.

However, while essential, effective rural infrastructure alone is not enough to assure agricultural and rural development and rapid increases in food production in developing countries. Yield enhancing production technology is of critical importance. Although opportunities for expansion of agricultural production into lands not currently under cultivation still exist in some countries, such opportunities are so limited that they would probably not be able to counter losses of current agricultural lands to alternative uses on a global level. Furthermore, attempts to expand agricultural production into new lands would, in most cases, require large investments in technology, tools and materials and would increase the risk of land degradation and deforestation. Thus, future increases in food production must come primarily from higher yields per unit of land rather than from land expansion.

Agricultural research has successfully developed yield-enhancing technology for the majority of crops grown in temperate zones and for several crops grown in tropical zones. The dramatic impact of agricultural research and modern technology on wheat and rice yields in Asia and Latin American since the mid-1980s is well known. Less dramatic but significant yield gains have been obtained from research and technological change in other crops, particularly maize.

Natural Resource Management and Environmental Considerations

Research, technology development, incentives, and regulations are needed to prevent environmental degradation. These measures include appropriate water management policies, reduction of subsidies that encourage wasteful use of inputs better definition of ownership and user rights to resources including land, education of farmers to encourage appropriate use of technology and resource conservation, and the provision of alternatives to resource-degrading inputs and techniques. Since poverty is a major source of degradation, poverty eradication is justified also on environmental grounds.

The recent surge in public and private concerns about negative environmental effects of economic growth and development may, if sustained, have important implications for agricultural development and future food production and consumption. Of particular concern of the need to avoid degradation of natural resources such as land and water, as well as deforestation, water contamination, and health risks associated with the use of chemicals. Since most of the current and potential resource degradation and environmental contamination result from situations in which those who cause and possibly benefit from degradation do not pay the costs, neither the market nor the individual producers and consumers are likely to incorporate preventive measures into their behaviour. Only when sufficient damage has been done to influence significantly current or future production costs will market and producer behaviour change. The state is more likely to undertake preventive measures either through publicly funded research and technology development or through incentive policies and regulations. Extensive water logging, salination, and associated land degradation and productivity losses resulting from inappropriate water management are of particular concern in large parts of Asia.

No Time for Complacency

Population growth will outstrip growth in food production in Sub-Saharan Africa for a long time to come unless more is done to accelerate agricultural growth. Between now and 2000, the population will grow at more than 3 per cent a year, while food production is likely to grow at 2 per cent or less a year. By the year 2000, the production shortfall is estimated to increase to about 50 million tons of grain equivalent, up from the current level of about 14 million tons. The region will not have the necessary foreign exchange to import such large amounts of food. And Africa governments will not be able to count on enough food aid to make up the difference. If current trends continue, by the year 2020, Africa will have a food shortage of 250 million tons, which is more than 20 times the current food gap.

Poverty is expected to increase rapidly in the coming years. Sub-Saharan Africa's share of the world's poor is expected to increase from the current 19 per cent to about 28 per cent in 2000. Furthermore, the number of underweight children in expected to increase in the 1990's in Sub-Saharan Africa.

Asian demand for cereals is estimated to grow at an annual rate of 2.1 per cent between now and the year 2000, where as food production is expected to grow at 1.9 per cent per year. Much of the production shortfall is likely to be dealt with through expanded imports and perhaps through expanded regional production in response to price increases.

In Latin America, by contrast, growth in food production is anticipated to exceed food demand growth: food production is estimated to grow by 3 per cent annually between 1990 and 2000, while food demand is estimated to grow by 2.5 per cent per year.

Large areas of land are rapidly being degraded and deforested. And the principal reasons for environmental degradation—poverty, high population growth, and limited access to appropriate agricultural technology—are not being dealt with effectively.

About 700 million people are food insecure for them the food crisis has arrived. For the 10-12 million preschool children who died in 1994 from hunger and diseases related to malnutrition, the food crisis came and went. One-third of the preschool children of the Third World are unable to grow to their full potential and face increased risk of death and disease.

Complacency is not in order. Clearly, Mathus underestimated the power of science to expand food production. The mass starvation that was predicted the Asia in the 1970s and 1980s did not occur because science was effectively put to work to expand crop yields. However, past yield increases came about people with foresight made appropriate decisions. The failure to expand investments in agricultural research and technology development during the 1980s and 1990s indicates that such foresight no longer prevails. Given the long lag time between investment in agricultural research and the resulting production increases, failure to invest today will show up in production shortfalls 10 to 20 years from now. The problems associated with environmental degradation will present themselves sooner. We must not wait until a global food crisis is upon us or until the last tree has fallen to make these investments.

REFERENCES

1. FAO, FAO Production Yearbook.
2. FAO, "The State of Food and Agriculture 1992".
3. FAO, "Agriculture Towards 2010".
4. FAO, "The State of Food and Agriculture 1994".
5. FAO, Food Outlook (December 1994).
6. World Bank, World Development Report 1995.
7. World Bank, Global Economic Prospects and the Developing Countries.
8. World Food Programme, Food Aid in Review (Rome WFP 1992).
9. World Bank, Global Economic Prospects and the Development Countries 1992. (Washington, D.C.: World Bank).

11

Irrigation Management: *Facing the Challenge*

Irrigation agriculture is up against an enormous challenge. India's population continues to grow at a tremendous rate. Over the next 10 years, there will be more extra mouths to feed. Water is becoming increasingly scarce for agriculture, with conflicting demands being made on limited supplies by the domestic and industrial sectors. The most attractive irrigation sites have already been exploited. Yet, irrigated agriculture will have to deliver average output increases of at least 3.5 per cent per year if future food demands are to be met in India.

Forty years ago in the 1950s and 1960s, India has worried about its capacity to produce sufficient food to feed its growing population. Episodes of food scarcity were not uncommon. It was dreaded that millions would die of hunger. Then dawned the miracle of the "green revolution". Cereal production increased by leaps and bounds, boosted by expanded irrigation, increased fertilizer application and modern crop varieties. The vigorous response in mobilizing financing towards boosting agricultural production paid off.

Given the importance of irrigation to the India's food supply and the vast resources already expanded on irrigation development, it is tragic that the actual performance of irrigation systems is so disappointingly low. In the post-green revolution era, it has become increasingly evident that the performance of irrigation systems, especially large-scale systems, is suboptimal whether measured in terms of achieving planning area targets or in terms of production potentials created by the physical works.

In many irrigation systems, the actual area irrigated is much less than the command area. Sharp inequities in water supplies between farmers in the head reaches of irrigation systems and those located downstream is another manifestation of poor performance. Investigations in the Tungbhadra Irrigation Scheme reveal that the tail-end of a major distributory commanding 25% of the total area, received approximately 20-40% of the targeted discharge while the upper reaches got more than their share.

Lack of maintenance has caused many systems to fall into disrepair, further inhibiting performance. Over time, distribution canals have become silted up, increasing the likelihood of breaching, damage to outlets and leading to salt build-up in the soil.

Successful Farmer-managed Irrigation Systems

Farmers have long demonstrated their potential capability to manage irrigation systems efficiently. Farmer-managed irrigation systems, (FMIS) also known as traditional, indigenous, communal or peoples' systems, are often classified "minor" or "small-scale" irrigation systems, although they may be found in command areas of 15,000-20,000 hectares.

Many successful farmer-managed irrigated systems, which have been functioning effectively for hundreds of years, represent a valuable, accumulated investment. They are also reservoirs of largely untapped irrigation management experience.

Research has revealed that FMIS contribute to the production of a significant portion of the subsistence food supply. Ground-water irrigation system, often found in areas affected by drought, play a strategic role in promoting food security. In India ground-water development which is increasing in importance is predominantly farmer-managed. In this country an estimated 20 million hectares are already under ground-water irrigation. When mismanaged though, ground-water irrigation could impact negatively on the environment.

In addition to the hectarage under farmer-managed ground-water irrigation, farmer-managed tank irrigation systems cover about 8.5 million hectares in this country. Farmer-managed irrigation systems have also allowed intensification of agriculture to partially meet the food needs of rapidly growing populations.

Little Awareness

Yet, despite the widespread interest in irrigation management turnover throughout India there is very little documentation about the processes used and the results obtained from irrigation management turnover. Many policy-makers do not know how to turn over management of their irrigation institutions in an effective way. They typically have very little, if any, awareness of the range of organisational options which may be suitable under different conditions. There is an urgent need, therefore, for a systematic, comparative assessment of the range of approaches being used, constraints to implementation and the impacts on performance of transferring management to non-governmental or farmers' organisations.

Successful irrigation in the future will be that which supports much higher levels of agricultural productivity, enhances responsiveness to more diversified and dynamic crop markets, stimulates more profitable irrigated agriculture for wide numbers of rural poor, substantially improves water use efficiency and supports the sustainable use of scarce land, biomass and water resources.

In the coming years the irrigation sector will be in ferment, with decision makers, agency managers and farmers needing better information and strategic processes to make intelligent choices in the management of irrigated agriculture.

12

Population Growth and Cropland

Since mid-century, global population has grown much faster than the cropland area. The trend is likely to continue in the next century, dropping cropland per person to historically low levels. The ever smaller per capita cropland base will make food self-sufficiency impossible for many countries, and will test the capacity of international markets to meet a growing demand for imported food.

For millennia, farmers satisfied rising food demand by bringing new land under the plow. But by mid-century cropland expansion could no longer meet the food needs of an increasingly populous and prosperous world. The 10,000 years era of steady expansion was over, and a new era began that stressed raising land productivity. As this high-yielding era shows signs of faltering, concern over the shrinking supply of cropland per person looms ever larger.

Since mid-century, grain area—which serves as a proxy for cropland in general—has increased by some 19 per cent, but global population has grown 132 per cent, seven times faster. Largely as a result, grain area per person has fallen by half since 1950, from 0.24 to 0.12 hectares. Assuming that grain area remains constant, grain area per person will fall to 0.07 hectares by 2050. In crowded industrial countries such as Japan, Taiwan, and South Korea, grain area per capita today is smaller than the area of a tennis court.

As grain area per person falls, more and more nations risk losing the capacity to feed themselves. Having already seen per capita grain area shrink by 40-50 per cent between

1960 and 1998, Pakistan, Nigeria, Ethiopia, and Iran can expect a further 60-70 per cent loss by 2050—a conservative projection that assumes no further losses of agricultural land. The result will be four countries with a combined population of more than 1 billion whose grain area per person will be only 300-600 square metres, less than a quarter of the area in 1950.

The historical record suggests that such a small area per person will send a substantial share of a country's people to world markets from their food. Consider the experience of six countries in East Asia whose per capita grain area currently ranges from 200 to 600 square metres per person. Sri Lanka relies on imports for more than a third of its grain, while Japan, Thiwan South Korea, and Malaysia buy more than 70 per cent of their grain form abroad. North Korea is the only one of the six that does not import heavily (it gets less than 20 per cent of its grain requirements from abroad), but its population is poorly fed-indeed, on the verge of starvation.

The concern is that population growth will push many nations—not just the four fastest-growing ones-below the 600-square meter-threshold in coming decades. In Asia alone, where grain area per person stands at 800 square metres, 16 countries are poised to cross this threshold by 2050, and many of them much sooner. As this process unfolds, the number of people who will turn to foreign markets for their food will likely jump sharply. These countries will find an increasingly tight international grain market, with nations from the Middle East, North Africa, and other regions already buying a third or more of their grain overseas.

In addition to per capita losses, population growth can lead to degradation of cropland, reducing its productivity or even eliminating it from production. As a country's population density increases and good farmland becomes scarece, poor farmers are forced onto ecologically vulnerable land such as hillsides and tropical forest. In the Philippines, for example, hillside agriculture accounted for only 10 per cent of all agricultural land in 1960, but 30 per cent in 1987. Because it is highly erodible, hillside land is easily damaged; worldwide, some 160 million hectares of hillside farmland—11 per cent of cropland—were characterized in 1989 as "severely eroded." Similarly, population pressure can force peasants to overfarm the poor soils of tropical forests. After being cleared and farmed for a few years, these soils typically require fallow periods of 20-25 years, but population pressures keep poor farmers on the same land for far langer than the soil can support, cutting fallow periods to just a few years in some areas of tropical Africa and Asia.

Finally, population pressures on a fixed base of land can result in rural landlessness. In Bangladesh, for example, landlessness among rural households, rose from 35 per cent in 1960 to 53 per cent in the early 1990s. Interestingly, Bangladesh is regarded as a success in slowing population expansion, as its growth rate declined from 2.8 per cent in the late 1970s to 1.5 per cent in the early 1990s. But its success came too late to prevent the increase in rural landlessness, highlighting the need to work sooner, rather than later, for population stabilisation.

13

Population Growth and Grain Production

The relationship between the growth in world population and the grain harvest has shifted over the last half-century, nearly dividing this period into two distinct eras. From 1950 to 1984, growth and the grain harvest easily exceeded that of population, raising the harvest per person from 247 kilograms to 342, a grain of 38 per cent. During the 14 years since then, growth in the grain harvest has fallen behind that of population, dropping output per person from its historic high in 1984 to an estimated 317 kilograms in 1998—a decline of 7 per cent, or 0.5 per cent a year.

These global trends conceal widely divergent developments among countries, contrasts that can be seen for the world's two most populous nations: India and China. In both, grain production per person was close to 200 kilograms as recently as 1978. Since then, the figure in India has edged up slightly but still falls short of 200 kilograms, while in China production has surged since the economic reforms in 1978, with per-person output now at nearly 300 kilograms. The combination of a dramatic surge in grain production and an equally dramatic reduction in population growth has given China a large margin of safety, effectively eliminating most of its hunger and malnutrition. Meanwhile, although India has also achieved impressive gains in its harvest, these have been largely cancelled by population growth, leaving its 976 million people living close to the margin.

What has happened in China and India is the story of developing countries in general. The overwhelming majority has achieved substantial, if not dramatic, gains in their grain harvests over the last half-century. Some, such as Thailand, have combined this with a much slower growth of population, which means that agricultural gains translate into rising grain production per person. In Pakistan, by contrast, grain production per person climbed steadily for awhile, but it peaked in 1981 at 186 kilograms. Since then it has been declining nearly 1 per cent a year. In effect, Pakistan's farmers are losing the battle with population growth.

The slower growth in the world grain harvest since 1984 is due to the lack of new land and to slower growth in irrigation and fertilizer use. Irrigated area per person, after expanding by 4 per cent since then as growth in the irrigated area has fallen behind that of population.

The increase in world fertilizer use has slowed dramatically since 1990, as diminishing returns to the application of additional fertilizer has stablized use in the United States, western Europe, and Japan and slowed annual growth in world fertilizer use from 6 per cent between 1950 and 1990 to scarcely 2 per cent in recent years.

Although Malthus was primarily concerned with the additional demand for grain generated by population growth, rising affluence is also playing a role. In a low income country such as India, grain consumption per person is less than 200 kilograms per year and diets are typically dominated by a single starchy staple-rice, for instance. With scarcely a pound of grain available a day per person, nearly all must be consumed directly, leaving little for conversion into animal protein. For the average American, on the other hand, the great bulk of the 800-kilogram daily grain consumption is taken in indirectly in the form of beef, pork, poultry, eggs, milk, cheese, ice cream, and yoghurt. At the intermediate level, in a country like Italy, people consume 400 kilograms of grain a day. Future food price stability thus depends on expanding production fast enough to keep up with both population growth and rising affluence.

One question often asked is, How many people can the Earth support? This must be answered with another question,

At what level of consumption? If the world grain harvest of 1.87 billion tons were expanded to 2 billion tons in the years ahead, it would support 10 billion Indians or 2.5 billion Americans. To answer the question of how many people the Earth can support, we first have to know the level of consumption we expect to live at.

Now that the frontiers of agricultural settlement have disappeared, future growth in grain production must come almost entirely from raising land productivity. Unfortunately, this is becoming more difficult. After rising at 2.1 per cent a year from 1950 to 1990, the annual increase in rain land productivity dropped to scarcely 1 per cent from 1990 to 1997. The challenge for the world's farmers is to reverse this decline at a time when cropland area per person is shrinking, the amount of irrigation water per person is dropping, and the crop yield response to additional fertilizer use is falling.

14

Population Growth and Meat Production

World meat production increased from 44 million tons almost twice as fast as population. In per capita terms, world meat production expanded from 17 kilograms in 1950 to 36 kilograms in 1997, more than doubling. Growth in meat production was originally concentrated in western industrial countries and Japan, but over the last two decades it has increased rapidly in East Asia (especially China), the Middle East, and Latin America.

When incomes begin to rise in traditional low-income societies, one of the first things people do is diversify their diets, consuming more livestock products. People everywhere appear to have an innate desire to consume at least moderate quantities of meat, perhaps reflecting our evolutionary history as hunter-gatherers.

Three types of meat—beef, pork, and poultry—account for the bulk of world consumption; mutton ranks a distant fourth. From 1950 until 1980, beef and pork production followed the same trend, but after the economic reforms in China—where pork is dominant—pork production surged ahead, climbing from 45 million tons to nearly 90 million tons in less than two decades.

Historically, growth in the world meat supply came primarily from beef and mutton, sustained by the world's rangelands. These areas, consisting mostly of land that is too arid to support crop production, cover a vast part of the planet, roughly double the cropland area. Not only do the herbs of cattle and flocks of sheep and goats provide meat and milk, but for millions of people in Africa, the Middle East, Central Asia, parts of the Indian subcontinent, and western China, they provide a livelihood. The only feasible way that this land can contribute to the world's food supply is to graze cattle, sheep, and goats on it, producing the meat and milk that directly and indirectly sustain large segment of humanity.

In recent years, beef and mutton production have levelled off at just over 60 million tons per year as the number of animals has pressed against the carrying capacity of range lands. With little unused grazing capacity left, future gains in meat production will have to come largely from feeding animals grain. At this point, the relative conversion efficiency of various animals begins to influence production trends. Producing a kilogram of beef in the feedlot requires roughly seven kilograms of grain, while a kilogram of pork requires nearly four of grain and a kilogram of poultry, just over two. As grain supplies tighten, the advantage shifts from beef to pork and even more so to poultry. This helps explain why world poultry production overtook that of beef in 1996.

Of the world grain harvest of 1.87 billion tons in 1998, an estimated 37 per cent or nearly 700 million tons—will be used to feed livestock and poultry, production milk and eggs as well as meat. This share, remarkably stable for the last decade, could go up or down depending on future grain prices.

Expanding world meat production also depends on soyabean production. If the grain fed to livestock or poultry is supplemented with a modest amount of soyabean meal (the high protein meal that is left after the oil is extracted), its conversion into meat is much more efficient. Largely as a result of this growing demand for livestock products, world soyabean production climbed from 17 million tons in 1950 to 152 million tons in 1997, a gain of ninefold.

To project the future demand for meat, we assume that the growth in meat consumption per person will slow over the next half-century, rising by one half instead of doubling, since some countries are nearing the saturation point. This, combined with the projected growth in population, would push total meat consumption from 211 million tons in 1997 to 513 million tons in 2050, a gain of 302 million tons. If we assume an average of 3 kilograms of grain per kilogram of meat produced, this would require more than 900 million tons of additional grain for feed in 2050, an amount equal to half of current world grain consumption. This would greatly intensify the competition between grain consumed directly and that consumed indirectly as animal protein, calling into question whether such gains in meat consumptions will ever materialize.

Grain fed to livestock and poultry is now the principal food reserve in the event of a world food emergency. As of 1990, the world had, in effect, three reserves in the global food system: substantial stocks of grain that could be drawn upon in the event of unexpected shortages, a large area of cropland idled under U.S. farm commodity programmes, and grain fed to animals. By 1998, world grain stocks had been depleted to one of the lowest levels on record and the cropland that was idled for half a century was returned to production. The only safety net remaining in the event of a major crop failure is the grain fed to livestock and poultry.

15

Watershed Development Programme

The Commissionerate of Rural Development is implementing area development programme i.e., watershed development programmes in dry and degraded lands through district agencies—DDP/DPAP/DWMA.

The programme of dry land development in Andhra Pradesh has undergone a major change from 1995-96, with the introduction of new participatory watershed guidelines based on the recommendations of Dr. Hanumantha Rao committee. The main emphasis of the revised guidelines is on active mobilisation and participation of the stakeholders in the programme at all stages—planning implementation and management. So far, out of 78.20 lakh ha. dry land to be treated by the Rural Development Department, 36.85 lakh ha. is treated/under treatment through 7903 watersheds/projects since 1995-96. The following watershed development programmes are being implemented in Andhra Pradesh:

1. Drought Prone Area Programme (DPAP)
2. Desert Development Programme (DDP)
3. Integrated Wastelands Development Programme (IWDP)
4. Employment Assurance Scheme (EAS)
5. Andhra Pradesh Hazard Mitigation (APHM)
6. Rural Infrastructure Development Fund (RIDF)

In order to combat the frequent recurrence of drought and for development of wasteland in the state, watershed programme is being implemented. A massive action plan for the development of all the degraded and wastelands in ten years was launched during 1996-97. Ten-year action plan has been prepared to develop 100 lakh hectares of degraded and wastelands on watershed basis with an outlay of about Rs. 4000.00 crores from 1997-2007 at the rate of 10 lakh hectares every year.

Andhra Pradesh is one of the few states in the country to have an exclusive administrative agency—DPAP/DDP/DWMA for the implementation of watershed development programme.

DPAP/DDP

Since 1995-96, 2966 DPAP and 552 DDP watershed projects are under implementation in Andhra Pradesh covering an area of 14.83 lakh ha. and 2.76 lakh ha. respectively (total = 17.59 lakh ha.).

291 DPAP and 110 DDP watershed projects are under implementation during 2002-03.

During 2003-04, action will be taken to cover more dry areas depending upon the projects to be sanctioned by the Govt. of India.

IWDP

Since 1995-96 842 watershed have been sanctioned upto December 2002 to develop 4.78 lakh ha. of wasterlands in Non-DPAP blocks under IWDP scheme.

108 watersheds have been sanctioned during 2002-03 upto December 2002 as against target of 144 watersheds under IWDP scheme.

During 2003-04, action will be taken to cover more dry areas depending upon the projects to be sanctioned by the Govt. of India.

EAS (Watersheds)

Since 1995-96, 1884 watersheds have been taken up covering an area of 9.42 lakh ha and component-wise action is being taken to complete them by March 2003.

RIDF VI

1244 RIDF watershed projects have been sanctioned to treat an area of 2.63 lakh ha. with Rs. 139.19 crores in 22 districts and we would complete all works by March 2004. The RIDF-VI projects have been sanctioned and 90 per cent as NABARD loan and 10 per cent GOAP share.

RIDF-VIII (RD and Others Sector)

NABARD has sanctioned 290 SMC project under RIDF VIII (RD and Others Sector) to cover an area of 1.48 lakh ha. with Rs. 41.08 crores to 17 districts with 75 per cent NABARD loan of Rs. 30.81 crores and 25 per cent of project cost with rice component of Rs. 10.27 crores during 2002-03.

APHM and ECRP

It is a World Bank assisted programme which commenced in July 1997 with a target of 100 watersheds @ 20 watersheds per district. The total area treated is 0.5 lakh ha. The project has been completed in July 2002.

Neeru-Meeru Programme

The Government of Andhra Pradesh has launched Neeru-Meeru programme with a view to converge efforts of all the departments involved in water conservation and management and to ensure large scale participation of people.

The programme was initiated on 01.05.2000 coinciding with 12th round of Janmabhoomi programme. Neeru-Meeru activities taken up by different departments are aimed at creating more filling space for harvesting rainwater which contributes to additional ground water recharge. Seven line departments (i.e., Rural Development, Forest, Minor Irrigation (I and CAD), Minor Irrigation (PR), Rural Water Supply (PR), Municipal Administration and Endowments) are actively involved in conservation and management of water resources.

Watershed Development Programme Performance and Impact

The performance of watershed programme in Andhra Pradesh is as follows:

Scheme-wise Watersheds

(From 1995-96 onwards) upto December 2002

S.No.	*Scheme*	*No. Water Sheds*	*Area under Treatment in Lakh ha.*
1.	DPAP	2966	14.93
2.	DDP	552	2.76
3.	IWDP	842	4.78
4.	EAS	1884	9.52
5.	APHM	100	0.50
6.	RIDF VI	1244	2.63
7.	RIDF VIII	290	1.48
8.	WDF	25	0.25
	Total	**7903**	**36.85**

Watershed projects under implementation : 7903

Land under watershed treatment : 36.85 lakh ha.

Amount invested on participatory watershed programme (upto December 2002) : Rs. 992.29 crores

Amount generated as people's contribution for watershed development fund : Rs. 49.61 crores

Impact

Andhra Pradesh State Remote Sensing Application Centre (APSRAC) is using satellite application and the satellite imageries are also used for evaluation. The Annual evaluation of watersheds in September 2002 has revealed the following impact and it shows that the programme is immensely useful to the farmers and the poor in dry areas.

1. No. of districts covered : 20
2. No. of watersheds evaluated : 5298

3.	Average increase in water levels (metres)	:	1.96
4.	Per cent of No. of wells rejuvenated	:	43%
5.	Additional area brought under cultivation (Ac.)	:	3,34,755
6.	Decrease in labour migration	:	61%
7.	Increase in milk production (ltrs. per day)	:	3,71,328
8.	Additional area brought under horticulture/afforestation(Ac)	:	3,56,046

D.P.A.P. Kurnool

Watershed Development Programme

1.	Total Geographical Area	17.63	lakhs ha.
2.	No. of Mandals	53	
3.	No. of Mandals Covered	48	
4.	No. of Habitations Covered	436	
5.	Total Area Included	4.40	lakh ha.
6.	No. of Micro Watersheds of 500 Ha. each	841	EAS-355
			IWDP-13
			DPAP-373
			APRLP-100
7.	No. of Project Implementing Agencies	71	
8.	No. of Govt. PIAs	48	
9.	No. of Non Govt. PIAs	23	
10.	No. of Watersheds Registered	841	
11.	No. of Watersheds Bank ACCTs opened	841	
12.	No. of User Groups	6071	
13.	No. of Self Help Groups	4095	

D.P.A.P., Kurnool

Physical and Financial Performance for 2002-03

Soil & Moisture Conservation

Sl. No.	*Name of the Scheme*	*Annual Target*		*Target upto December' 02*		*Achievement Upto December' 02*		*Balance*	
		Phy.	*Fin.*	*Phy.*	*Fin*	*Phy.*	*Fin.*	*Phy.*	*Fin.*
1.	DPAP	3053	67.863	2291	39.683	2048	28.372	762	28.181
2.	EAS	5114	113.687	3838	66.477	3317	45.938	1276	47.209
3.	RIDF-VI								
4.	RIDF-VIII								
	Total	**8167**	**181.550**	**6129**	**106.160**	**5365**	**74.310**	**2038**	**75.390**

(Contd...)

Contd...

Water Harvesting Structures

Sl. No.	Name of the Scheme	Annual Target		Target upto December 02		Achievement Upto December 02		Balance	
		Phy.	Fin.	Phy.	Fin	Phy.	Fin.	Phy.	Fin.
1.	DPAP	5310	457.154	3983	368.335	11349	442.010	1327	88.819
2.	EAS	7315	266.926	5255	283.225	16233	360.558	2060	27.521
3.	RIDF-VI	568	425.780	406	280.690	1012	304.510	162	121.270
4.	RIDF-VIII	1012	53.130	1012	53.130	1132	50.622	0	0.000
	Total	14205	1222.990	10656	985.380	29726	1157.700	3549	237.610

Contd...

Sl. No.	Name of the Scheme	Afforestration and Horticulture							
		Annual Target		Target upto December' 02		Achievement Upto December' 02		Balance	
		Phy.	Fin.	Phy.	Fin	Phy.	Fin.	Phy.	Fin.
1.	DPAP	3686	197.108	3686	118.965	4995	96.025	0	78.143
2.	EAS	5725	272.351	5725	141.443	7639	97.631	0	130.907
3.	RIDF-VI	450	57.851	450	57.851	450	57.851	0	0.000
4.	RIDF-VIII								
	Total	**9861**	**527.310**	**9861**	**318.259**	**13084**	**251.507**	**0**	**209.050**

(Contd...)

Contd...

		Trainings, Comm. Org. & Est.				Toral			
Sl. No.	Name of the Scheme	Annual Target	Target. Upto December' 02	Achievement Upto December' 02	Balance	Annual Target	Target Upto December' 02	Achievement Upto December' 02	Balance
1.	DPAP	114.794	86.094	62.951	26.700	836.919	613.077	629.358	223.843
2.	EAS	192.306	144.226	101.926	48.080	865.270	635.371	606.053	253.717
3.	RIDF-VI					483.631	338.541	362.361	121.270
4.	RIDF-VIII					53.130	53.130	50.622	0.000
	Total	**307.100**	**230.320**	**164.877**	**76.780**	**2238.950**	**1640.119**	**1648.394**	**598.830**

Watershed Development Programme—Kurnool District

	Total Watersheds	841
(a)	Completed	260
(b)	Ongoing	581
	Mandals covered	48
	Villages covered	436
	Area covered (lakh ha.)	4.40

16

Development of Sericulture

In majority of the developing nations, development efforts in the last decade were put on hold. In all the developing nations, poverty is on rise, economic growth has slowed down, employment has faltered and inflation is on upward swing. A greater proportion of the population in these countries depends on agriculture sector for their livelihood. But, in agriculture sector productivity is low. This is not only because of excess pressure on land but also agriculture in these developing nations is characterised by primitive technologies, poor organisation and limited capital.

Since the urban growth is severely limited, the growing labour forces have to get their employment in the rural areas or semi-urban areas in the coming decades. So, it has become compulsory for the agriculture sector to share the increasing burden since it is the major activity for the majority of the labour force.

It is obvious that in India larger than the necessary number of workers needed in agriculture are working on limited resources. As a result, agriculture sector has become an unprofitable activity with low levels of productivity. Moreover, the traditional crops have failed to absorb the growing labour force and to raise the incomes of the farmers above the subsistence level.

Since agriculture has been considered as the backbone of Indian economy, Indian agriculture can be broadly classified under two categories—(1) rainfed or dryland farming and (2) irrigated farming. Rainfed agriculture is primarily rain dependent. Rainfed agriculture in India supports 40 per cent of the total cultivated area. As irrigation facilities are inadequate, agriculture is still a gamble in the hands of monsoons.

For most of the irrigation projects, rainfall is the only source. Due to erratic nature of rainfall, most of the dams, tanks and other water reservoirs remain dry but also at the stage of rearing of silk worms using output of the farmers as an input of the latter. Sericulture, for example, played a very important rule in transforming the traditional bound Japanese agriculture into a modernised agriculture by intensive use of land, labour and capital.

Now, in India sericulture has become the most promising rural activity due to certain specific reasons like minimum gestation period, less investment, maximum employment potential and quick turnover of the investment. Sericulture generates direct and indirect employment in various ways. First, mulberry cultivation creates employment on the farm and secondly cocoon production which uses mulberry leaves as an input creates large-scale employment for the family labour of the mulberry growers, if that operation is also undertaken by the same household to reduce their underemployment in agriculture. Further, the reeling activity is also mainly undertaken in rural areas or semi-urban areas and the employment generated there would help to reduce the rural unemployment in a significant way. In short, sericulture as a whole, by its very nature of activities creates large scale employment and income generation opportunities in the rural and nearby semi-urban areas accelerating the economic growth of these areas.

Details of Sericulture Development in Kurnool District of A.P.

Sericulture is better suited for drought prone areas. Kurnool district is one among the frequently drought affected district of Ryalaseema and suitably sericulture finds its place. Sericulture was first introduced in the district during 1975-76 in Bapananthapuram village of Atmakur Mandal. The area under mulberry was gradually increased over the years to

10,000 acres covering almost in all mandals in the district upto 1990 and the area stood at all-time high in 1990. But in the subsequent years the net area got reduced because of large scale uprooting by existing farmers due to losses suffered by them an account of steep fall in cocoon price and outbreak of deadly chronic disease in 1991/92 scanty erratic rains and continuous dry spell also major factors for uprooting. However due to its during summer season. These rainfed areas are frequently affected by periodic droughts, soil erosion, crop fluctuations and other related problems. To overcome these problems, the Government of India has implemented such projects which are helpful for eradication of poverty and unemployment and upliftment of the weaker sections.

In the context suitable strategies are needed to overcome the above mentioned problems. The discovery of productive employment opportunities in the integrated rural development assumes vital importance in the economic development of India. So, it is natural to start with agriculture as the biggest of India's industries. The most important method of securing an increase in agriculture output is by inducing the cultivators to adopt better agricultural practices.

In fact, Indian agriculture now is no longer confined to the cultivation of traditional crops. The farmers are encouraged to take up agriculture practices which are integrated with live-stock culture, animal husbandry, dairying, fisheries, poultry, horticulture and sericulture to generate more income for each household.

In spite of the limitations in agriculture, it can be said without any doubt that Indian agriculture is on the threshold of entering into a stage of development characterised by a shift from static technology to a modern technology, in which capital requirement and purchased inputs occupy a larger share. But, much of the success of new programmes will depend upon the ability of the workers who act as growth promoters.

It is in this context, sericulture with its vast potential for employment generation in rural areas plays a vital role in alleviating rural areas plays a vital role in alleviating rural

Item	*1994-95*	*1995-96*	*1996-97*	*1997-98*	*1998-99*	*1999-2000*	*2000 to 2001 as on 1/2001*
Area under mulberry ultivation Acres	4930	5273	5141	4232	5115	4195	3952
Cocoon production (in tonnes)·	882	895	967	924	107	7.66	6.15
Qty. of raw silk produced both in Pvt. and Govt. Sectors (in Tonnes	2.23	2.2	3.8	6.0	3.3	3.3	4.3
	2450	2649	2774	2386	2558	2131	1935

poverty. However, this is another crop enterprise which is identified as one of the most appropriate labour intensive cottage industries. This activity combines both agriculture and industry. It provides gainful employment not only at the stage of raising of mulberry plants lucrative income the area under mulberry is developed. Now the district is self sufficient and even supplying seed cocoon to neighbouring districts. As for non-farm sector in sericulture in the district one 6 basin multiend silk reeling unit. One 6 basin silk reeling unit and 40 country charkas and a complex of 100 Twin Charkas are established in private sector. As many as 3,00 silk looms are functioning in Adoni area.

6. Infrastructure facilities available in the district:

Govt. Sector

1.	Tech. service Centers Extension)	:	7 Nos. (Atmakur, Pamulpadu, M. Lingapuram, Nandyal, Nandikotkur, Adoni and Pathikonda.
2.	Tech. Service Centre (Non-Farm)	:	1 No. (Atmakur)
3.	Govt. Silk Reeling Unit	:	1 No. (Kurnool)
4.	Silk worm egg Production centers	:	2 nos. (Atmakur, Nandyal)
5.	Govt. Seed Farms	:	5 Nos. (Peapully, Kalichetla, Venkatapuram, Gajulapalli and Thangadancha)
6.	Seed Areas	:	2 Nos. (Adoni, Peapully)
7.	Govt. Seed Concoon Market	:	1 No. (Adoni)
8.	Govt. CB Cocoon Market	:	1 No. (Atmakur)

Private Sector

1.	Pvt. Charkas	:	4 Nos. Nandikotkur, Atmakur
2.	Silk Twisting Units	:	4 Nos. Yemmiganur, Kodumur Nandikotkur and Nandyal
1.	Silk Power loom Units	:	1 No. Yemmiganur

2. Silk Looms: 3118 Nos. Kodumur, Yemmiganur, Adoni, Pathikonda, Koilakuntla Nandavaram

3. Silk Weavers Co-Op Society : 1 No. Gudikal (with 40 looms)

4. Details of loans and subsidies (Credit Flow):

Sl. No.	*Item*	*1996-97*		*1997-98*		*1998-99*		*1999-2000*	
1.	Loan	23.7	17.80	2.61	—	0.69	—	—	—
2.	Subsidy	8.78	7.13	5.12	—	0.46	—	—	—
3.	Margin Money	—	1.78	—	—	—	—	—	—
	Total	32.50	26.7	7.73	—	1.15	—	—	—

8. Achievements under VIII plan: Provided 100 House-cum-Work Sheds for Charka Silk Reeling to the rural poor people.

9. Proposals under IX Plan

(a) Providing rearing sheds on 50% subsidy to Seed Farms by CSB

(b) Providing Drip irrigation to Mulberry gardens of seiculturists

(c) Establishment of Multiend Silk Reeling Machine's

10. Women Development Programme

Sl. No.	*Year*	*Programme*	*Physical*	*Financial*
1.	1995-96	1. Women Farmers Meet	350	
		2. Women Groups	02	
		3. Thrift-Cum-Credit Group	02	
2.	1996-97	1. Study Tours	125	0.4375
		2. Try in Mulberry Cultivation's & SW Rearing	25	0.1125
		3. Women Groups	02	0.50

(Contd...)

3.	1997-98	1.	Try to women Sericulturists in New Technologies	75 —	0.225 —
		2.	Women Groups	01	0.25
4.	1998-99	1.	Trg. to Women sericulturists in New techniques.	30	0.30
		2	Women Groups	01	0.25
5.	1999-2000		Nil	—	—
6.	2000-2001		Nil	—	—

Trends in Employment under Sericulture

Year	*No. of Persons engaged in sericulture*
1995-96	19076
1996-97	20564
1997-98	16928
1998-99	20460

12. Cocoons Markets in the District

1. Atmakur: : CB Cocon Market
2. Kurnool : Notified Cocoon Market
3. Adoni : Seed Cocoon Market

13. Transactions Made in Govt. Cocoon Markets

Year	*Qty. of Cocoons sold*	*Market fee collected*	*Total value realised*
1995-96	5429	11904	566744
1996-97	6973	17518	822714
1997-98	11748	25892	1294000
1998-99	4458	8276	489000
1999-2000	137390	28999	1449886
2000-2001	1034	20463	1271947

17

Solving Conflicts Over Water Uses

There are few issues that have greater impact on the life of mankind and the planet as a whole than the management of our most important natural resource water. This has only been realized in detail more recently by the general public as well as by many planners and decision-makers. Around the world they have begun to appreciate the critical importance of a reliable water supply for their future survival and sustainable development. Rivers are lifelines in countries like India serving different uses such as transport, agriculture, fisheries, personal hygiene and others. Conflicts over use of water resources must be settled through better water management policies.

In many localities of the Earth water-related problems have become extremely acute, even critical. In some places they are the source of social instability and are a threat to international security. There is not the slightest doubt that, with further population increase and under the "water business-as-usual" scenario, these problems will become ever major acute, thus creating ever more instability. After decades of water waste, water pollution, and inability to provide basic water services to the poor we must fundamentally change the way we think about and manage water. We have to realise that water can no longer be considered to be a cheap and plentiful resource, which can be used abused or squandered without much concern for further human welfare.

As fresh water is becoming scarce, that is when there is not enough water to satisfy all demands, competition develops.

Besides the well known tensions at international level over limited water supplies there is an-increasing and in many cases a far more important competition over water arising within countries, between sectors. Such competition, for instance, occurs between farmers for irrigation water and between farmers and non-agricultural users of water such as cities (including industries and power plants) and environmental concerns (recreation, fish and other wildlife). Because of this increasing competition irrigated agriculture around the world, but especially in developing countries, faces important challenges in the coming decades, on the one hand, it has to provide a major share of the required increases in food and fiber production to meet the objectives of poverty alleviation and development. On the other hand. It is threatened by water shortages arising out of increasing competition from domestic, industrial and other sectors. This situation is further worsened by dwindling financial resources available for capital expenditure as the cost of new irrigation schemes increase.

Land under Irrigation

On a regional basis, it is estimated that for example around 60 per cent of the value of crop production in Asia is grown on irrigated land. The irrigated sector performs an essential task in meeting the basic food needs of billions of people. It has provided more than half of the two most important basic staples and close to a third of all food crops. In the future, the irrigated sector will have to provide an even larger proportion of the total food output. The questions arises whether irrigated agriculture will be in the position to provide the extra food needed to feed a growing population despite an increasing water scarcity and inter sectoral competition. There is no general, no easy answer to this question. But the following implications are foreseeable.

The irrigation sector has to recognise that economic structures are dynamic and not static. The economics of many countries have undergone considerable change in the last decades. In connection with this change agriculture is losing its leading role in economic development and this is, besides other things, affecting the allocation of water resources between agriculture and other users. The same applies to many other countries around the world, especially developing countries in arid and semi-arid climates.

New Water Policies are Needed

Because of the growing competition for ever-scarcer water resources governments, and water authorities are forced to change water policies. Objectives of the new policies are demand-decreasing and demand-shifting. Irrigated agriculture, by far the dominant water user, will be strongly effected by such policy changes.

Water has an economic value in all its competing uses and should be recognised as an economic good. Agriculture will in future not any more get water free of charge as it did in the past. Farmers will have to pay for the water, and costs will be increasing steadily over the years to come.

There will be a reduction of the role of governments in rural water projects and an increasing importance of local user groups. Experience shows that an important solution to water related problems is to give users the responsibility for developing and managing the water resource. This requires that farmers become properly organised in water user associations able to discharge their new responsibilities, and that they have security of tenure to the land they farm and irrigate.

During the recent decade growth in crop productivity in irrigated areas has slowed, and competition for water for non-agricultural uses has increased. These developments place strong demands to develop water resource policies to maintain growth in irrigated agricultural production:

- facilitate efficient allocation of water across sectors and final demands; and
- reverse the ongoing degradation of the water resource base, including the watershed irrigated land base, and water quality.

What water policies can lead to efficient increases in irrigated production while reducing resource degradation in the irrigated areas in developing countries and releasing water for growing non-agricultural demands? What policies can be implemented to conserve water in non-agricultural uses to reduce competition between sectors?

Questions to be Answered

Among other the following questions still have to be answered:

1. What are the implications of growing competition between agricultural and non-agricultural uses of water for the availability and productivity of water in agriculture?

2. How to use regulations, water prices, pollution taxes and effluent charges to encourage water conservation and pollution control in industries and households?

3. What are the production, equity, employment generation and income impacts of alternative water allocation mechanisms in different agroeconomic and scarcity environments? What investment and administrative costs are associated with different mechanisms? What is the impact of resource allocation methods on water use, cropping patterns, crop yields, and fertilizer and other input use, capital investments, farm income, and environmental degradation?

4. What is the connection between alternative allocative mechanisms and the environmental externalities caused by irrigation, including water logging, salinisation, ground water recharge and ground water mining?

5. How will food security in low income countries be effected by changing water policies?

In the context of the growing competition for water it is important to enable policy makers to evolve a policy-mix which will result in efficient, equitable and environmentally sustainable allocation of water resources to user sectors. To achieve this, extensive research work is needed.

18

End of Controversy on Large Dams?

Was it worth the effort? The energy, the time, the money invested? Quite a number of people probably put this question to themselves on the 16th of November 2000 when Nelson Mandela launched the final report of the World Commission on Dams (WCD) in London. In an extraordinary process that lasted two and a half years, dam proponents and opponents worked intensely together. Twelve commissioners had tried hard to come up with a consensus on the effects of large dams in the past, and with recommendations for future sustainable planning on water and energy issues. And surprisingly enough: the Commission succeeded. The cost of ten million dollars was financed by governments, international agencies, the private sector, NGOs and various foundations—this is also a novelty. Dam-affected people, non-governmental organisations, companies, consultants, politicians etc. contributed to the processes with their know-how and by giving support and additional resources to the Commission's work.

The establishment of the multi-stakesholder Commission was the result of a growing and aggravating controversy about the social, ecological and often enough also economic costs of large dams.

Global Review Shows Faulty Planning Processes

The WCD Global Review of large dams proves that there were good reasons for massive resistance against large dams in the past. As the report says: "In too many cases an unacceptable price has been paid... especially in social and environmental terms, by people displaced, by communities downstream, by taxpayers and by the natural environment" While funders of large dams, political institutions, consultants and companies claimed in recent years that they had learned from their faults and improved their performance, the WCD highlights that, while policies and assessment procedures have been improved, it appears that business-as-usual too often continued to prevail.

- Even in the 1990s, impacts on downstream livelihoods were not adequately assessed or accounted for in the planning and design of large dams.
- Participation and transparency in planning processes for large dams was neither inclusive nor open, and while actual change in practice remains slow, even in the 1990s, there is increasing recognition of the importance of inclusive processes.
- Where opportunities for the participation of affected people and the undertaking of environmental and social impact assessment have been provided they often occur late in the process, are limited in scope and even in the 1990s their influence in project selection remains marginal.

Dams Hindered Human Development

The WCD states that "dams have made an important and significant contribution to human development, and the benefits derived from them have been considerable". A viewpoint that dam-affected people and NGOs hardly share, having in mind the experiences of the past. Medha Patkar, WCD Commissioner and activist in the struggle to save the Narmada river in India wrote in her comment to the Report: "Within the value framework the Commission propagates—equity, sustainability, transparency, accountability, participatory decision-making and efficiency—large dams have not helped attain, but rather hindered 'human development'.

The WCD also puts an end to the old viewpoint that the violation of human rights and the social costs that some have to pay can be justified by the benefits for the others. The idea that society as a whole would profit from so-called development that were benefiting from 'trickle down effect'. In fact this development model tends to aggravate social inequities and encourage environmental destruction leaving the rich better off, but the poor more magnialised and resentful. It is not a sustainable model.

It's Not Just About Dams

Although it is called the World Commission on Dams the issues before the Commission are much broader. The discussion about large dams is inevitably linked with the need to find solutions for supplying water and energy in the future. To do this in a sustainable way is one of the challenges of our time.

The WCD defined 5 core values that are based on internationally accepted norms like the Universal Declaration of Human Right to Development and the Rio Declaration on environment and Development:

- Equity
- Efficiency
- Participatory decision-making and Accountability

These values are not really new and some of them have been agreed upon decades ago, but the Global Review of the WCD showed that 'in real life' we are still far from implementing them.

The rights and risks approach of the WCD must be mentioned as an important tool: while founders and dam-builders talk a lot about their (mostly) financial risks, risks of the dam-affected people were not a big issue in the past. The Commission makes an important distinction: while the former take a voluntary risk and have the possibility to decide on whether or not they want to take it, the latter take involuntary risks and so far had hardly any option in deciding on whether or not they are willing to incur them. Rights must not be violated in order to serve the needs of other people. Respecting human rights is the minimum basis for discussion and is not negotiable.

To get better results in the future the WCD defined seven strategic priorities for decision-making:

- Gaining Public Acceptance
- Comprehensive Options Assessment
- Addressing Existing Dams
- Sustaining Rivers and Livelihoods
- Recognising Entitlements and Sharing Benefits
- Ensuring Compliance
- Sharing Rivers for Peace, Development and Security

According to the WCD there are several fundamental strategic points in the decision-making process. One point is right at the beginning of the planning stage: if the discussion about sustainable energy and resources management is carried out in a transparent, open and participatory process, further steps are much more likely to be accepted by all parties and will help prevent conflicts at later project stages. According to the WCD there are several fundamental strategic points in the decision making process. One point is right at the beginning of the planning stage: if the discussion about sustainable energy and resources management is carried out in a transparent, open and participatory process, further steps are much more likely to be accepted by all parties and will help prevent conflicts at later project stages.

The strategic priority "Addressing existing dams' includes (among other policy principles) the identification and assessment of outstanding social issues associated with existing large dams. Considering that between 40 to 80 million people have been displaced by large dams (a lot more have been directly or indirectly affected) this is a difficult task. Financial institutions, development agencies and companies are a lot more interested in looking at the future than dealing with the complex problems of the past. But there is no way out. Dam-affected people of the past along with future dam-affected people are unlikely to accept new dams and believe in what is being promised while the legacy of the past is being forgotten. To solve these problems is a condition for further constructive discussions if not a mere moral obligation. How can those responsible for planning future dams think of gaining public acceptance if not by showing that they mean what they say?

The recommendations of the WCD are of fundamental importance, because they were agreed upon in a multi-stakeholder process. In other words, they were made by representative of industry as well as those from dam-affected people, by members coming from industrialized countries as well as those from developing countries. Within the Commission, it was possible to integrate the most diverse views and to come to a consensus.

No More Dams?

Although in their assessment the evidence would have allowed even stronger recommendations, NGOs and people's movements welcomed the report and asked for immediate implementation. Other stakeholders do not seem to be very enthusiastic about it. Quite a few representatives from industry and investors seem to fear that the implementaiton of the WCD recommendations would lead to an abrupt stop in dam building.

All appreciate that the WCD report vindicates many concerns raised by NGO campaigns. Given the role of financial institutions in funding large dams and in the WCD process, and based on the WCD report's recommendations, all has to call on all public financial institutions, including the World Bank, the regional development banks, the export credit agencies an bilateral aid agencies, to take the following actions:

- All public financial institutions should immediately and comprehensively adopt the recommendations of the World Commission on Dams, and should integrate them into their relevant policies, in particular those on water and energy development, environmental impact assessment, resettlement, and public participation. In particular, as recommended by the

WCD, no project should proceed without the free, prior and informed consent of indigenous people, and without the demonstrable acceptance of all those who would be affected by the project.

- All public financial institutions should immediately establish independent transparent and participatory reviews of all their planned and ongoing dam projects. While such reviews are taking place, project preparation and construction should be halted. Such reviews should establish whether the respective dams comply, as a minimum, with the recommendations of the WCD. If they do not, projects should be modified accordingly or stopped altogether.
- All institutions which share in the responsibility for the unresolved negative impacts of dams should immediately initiate a process to establish and fund mechanisms to provide reparations to affected communities that have suffered social, cultural and economic harm as a result of dam projects.
- All public financial institutions should place a moratorium on funding the planning or construction of new dams until they can demonstrate that they have complied with the above measures.

19

Controlling the Global Tobacco Epidemic Towards a Transnational Response

Recent trends in the globalisation of the tobaco industry are reflected in the shifting of the burden of tobaco-related disease and deaths towards developing countries. Tobaco companies have proved sufficiently powerful to thwart comprehensive control programmes in all but a handful of countries. What new strategies are needed to control the epidemic in developing regions?

One billion people smoke world-wide and around 3.5 million die from tobacco-related illnesses annually. By 2030, this figure will rise to ten million, with 70 per cent of deaths in lower and middle income countries (LMICs). Four companies now control 75 per cent of global cigarette sales, as sophisticated strategies for supply production and sales have produced increasingly popular global brands.

The onward march of Marlboro man epitomises this globalisation, exploiting the opportunities presented by trade liberalisation, regional organisations and the communications revolution. Control efforts are undermined by the industry's success in developing favourable relationships with many governments, the magnitude of their foreign direct investments and the scale of advertising, marketing and sponsorship campaigns. In addition, large-scale cigarette smuggling, which comprises one-third of total exports, depletes tax revenues and further jeopardises public health.

A unique response by the World Health Organisation (WHO) reflects the scale of the challenge. WHO is negotiating its first public health treaty: the Framework Convention on Tobaco Control. To be effective, this potentially powerful instrument must be backed up by strengthened national policies set within the context of globalisation and based on an appreciation of transnational tobaco industry strategies. In support of this process, an international team based at the London School of Hygiene and Tropical Medicine carried out pilot studies in Thailand and Zimbabwe. These aimed to initiate the development of guidelines for tobacco policy research in LMICs, where resources and expertise are frequently lacking.

The political sensitivities surrounding tobaco control reflect the complex array of powerful vested interests involved. The case studies showed that political mapping and stakeholder analysis can make a valuable contribution to understanding the opportunities and constraints for national control policies in an era of globalisation. For example, they found that the 1992 Global Agreement on Tariffs and Trade (GATT) ruling that opened Thailand's previously closed cigarette market had contradictory results:

- Thailand is a key market for tobacco companies seeking expansion in Asia.
- The US Trade Representatives secured access to the Thai market through GATT's insistence on equal treatment of domestic and foreign cigarette manufacturers, and imports escalated rapidly.
- The GATT ruling also upheld the right to protect public health, giving a major impetus to health activists pressing the Thai government for action.
- Subsequent comprehensive control legislation has stablished smoking rates in Thailand.

Control polices of wealthier countries cannot simply be transplanted to poorer nations. Knowledge of the complex policy environments surrounding tobacco control in LMICs is limited and effective policies will require.

- detailed analysis of the particular political and economic contexts.

- multidisciplinary expertise from public health and social science.
- Links between researchers, policymakers and activists.
- Support for national research capacity through the development of clear guidelines for tobacco policy analysis and their application by national researchers.

Finally, the enforced opening of internal industry documents provides an important new resource. Access to the depositories in Minnesota, USA, and Guildford, UK, and via the internet offers a unique opportunity to understand the global strategies of the tobacco companies. Analysis of their contents has so far focused on the United States. There is an urgent need to extend this attention to industry activities within LMICs.

20

A Breakthrough in the Evolution of Large Dams?

Back to the Negotiating Table

"The problem is not the dams. It is the hunger. It is the thirst. It is the darkness in a township". With these plain words, former South African President Nelson Mandela summed up the World Commission on Dams (WCD's) motives in a speech at the presentation praising its work. His position is similar to that of the many other representatives of the South who were present: he demands a right to development. But Ms Medha Patkar, of India, a WCD Commission member and founder of the Struggle to Save the Narmada River (Narmada Bachao Andolan) anti-dam movement, takes a contrary view. "The problems of the dams are only a symptom of the larger failure of the unjust and destructive dominant development model," she says. We need to challenge "the forces that lead to the marginalisation of a majority through the imposition of unjust technologies like large dams".

Stagnation in Dam Building

The WCD is a unique experiment in reaching consensus. It began in April 1997 when with the support of the World Bank and the World Conversation Union (IUCN), 39 representative of diverse interests met at a workshop in Gland, Switzerland. At this point the various positions of the participants from governments, the private sector, international financial institutions, civil society Organisations and affected people were cast in stone. The Manibeli

Declaration in June 1994 of 326 activist groups from 44 countries had called for an immediate moratorium on World Bank funded large dams until a comprehensive, independent review of all Bank funded projects had been conducted. International financial institutions were actually no longer able to fund further large dams in the face of public criticism. Enervated by steadily growing protests despite continual tightening of social and environmental standards, the institutions' representatives wearily likened the dispute to a football match in which somebody kept moving the goalposts. But one proposal to emerge from the meeting in Gland was for all parties to work together in establishing the World Commission on Dams.

The WCD began its work in May 1998 under the chairmanship of Prof. Kader Asmal, then South Africa's Minister of Water Affairs and Forestry. Its 12 members were chosen to reflect regional diversity, expertise and stakeholder perspectives. But the Commission ran the risk of failure right from the start due to their confrontational attitudes. The members, who spent 2 years 6 months jointly organising hearings, consultations and case studies and analysing more than 100 existing large dams, could not be more disparate.

The Current Situation

A large dam is a dam with the height of 15 m or more from the foundation. If dams are 5-15 metres high and have a reservoir volume of more than three million cubic metres, they are also classified as large dams. Using this definition, there are more than 45,000 large dams around the world, almost half of them in China. They were built in the 20th century to meet the constantly growing demand for water and electricity. On a global scale, hydropower dams account for about 20 per cent of electricity generated, and in 24 countries, including Brazil, Democratic Republic of Congo, Zambia and Norway, hydropower covers more than 90 per cent of national electricity supply needs. Half the world's large dams were built solely or mainly for irrigation. Between 12 per cent and 16 per cent of world food production is based on dams, and as reservoirs they provide protection against floods.

Unfortunately, this impressive balance is counteracted by comparably significant problems. Construction of large dams is a major intervention in the ecosystem of rivers and the lives of many people. The WCD estimates that some 40-80 million people, mostly indigenous peoples, have been displaced by reservoirs worldwide and robbed of their livelihoods from fishing or farming. Serious conflicts are simmering between neighbouring countries because dams have turned off the water supply for downstream states.

The late Indian Prime Minister Jawaharlal Nehru once said: "Dams are India's new temples." Right up to the 1970s, large dams were seen as the synonym for development and economic progress. Dam-building reached its peak between 1970 and 1980, when an average of two to three new large dams per day were commissioned. But a considerable number of the dams analysed by the WCD have fallen short of their technical and economic objectives. Construction cost overruns averaged 56 per cent. Many dams have had negative ecological impacts, and the disadvantages for people living downstream were mostly not taken into account. The planning of dams did not examine sufficiently possible alternatives for meeting power and water needs. There were hardly any retrospective evaluations of dam projects.

A New Framework for Decision-making?

Despite this sobering stocktaking, the WCD arrives at an astonishingly simple finding: dams are primarily a means to an end. Their task is to improve the well-being of the people on a sustainable basis. This improvement should be economically acceptable, socially just and environmentally sound. If this goal can be achieved by a dam, its construction should be supported. Where alternative options offer a better solution they should be the preferred choice.

The Commission based its work on a set of five crore values for future decision-making: equity, efficiency, participatory decision-making, sustainability, and accountability. With regard to legal aspects and the extent of the potential risks for those involved, the WCD proposes development of an approach based on recognising rights and assessing risks. All risk-bearers should have a place at the negotiating table.

The WCD also recommends seven strategic priorities for decision-making: gaining public acceptance; comprehensive options assessment; reviewing existing dams; sustaining rivers and livelihoods; recognising entitlements and sharing benefits; ensuring compliance; and sharing rivers for peace, development and security. These priorities are reinforced by 23 practical criteria and guidelines which can be adopted, adapted and applied by all actors involved in the dam controversy. For instance, the WCD suggests analysing points at issue together with the people affected by existing dams and developing joint proposals for solutions. People affected by new dam projects should be among their favoured beneficiaries, and their claims should be made legally binding.

The report offers a comprehensive compilation of knowledge, which previously was limited to individual case studies or a narrow specialist context, on the social, economic, technological and ecological problems and impacts of large dams. That makes the report a central reference which helps greatly in bringing objectivity into the debate. Provision of an analytical framework and strategic options is certainly an important step. But with regard to its task of developing internationally valid criteria and guidelines for the planning, design, appraisal, building operation, monitoring and shutdown of dams, the report remains very general. What will be decisive here will be to practice with the relevant actors the method and content of the suggested mediation process on the basis of specific cases.

Deeds Must Follow Words

The WCD's work must now be made useable for the private sector, civil society and development purpose. What is required is a discussion process involving all major actors. The objective of this process must be the development of practical and effective guidelines in addition to the current standards.

The WCD calls on bilateral development organisations and multilateral development banks to support only dam projects that have resulted from an open process of examining various options. The parties should observe the WCD guidelines. Measures to save water and power should be examined and, if applicable, be promoted.

Private sector companies should publish guidelines on corporate behaviour and knowledge the WCD principles, criteria and guidelines. Further, the private sector should draw up and implement voluntary codes of conduct, management systems and certification procedures, such as the internationally recognized standard for environmental management (ISO 14001). The OECD's Anti-Corruption Agreement should be observed, and declarations of honesty incorporated in contracts. Business associations should develop processes to monitor compliance with the WCD guidelines.

NGOs should primarily check compliance with agreements and assist aggrieved parties to seek compensation. They should also assist in identifying relevant stakeholders for dam projects, using the rights and risks approach. Finally the NGOs should build up support networks and partnerships between them.

Importance of Information

But do these noble proposals provide the whole answer? The WCD process is based on the opportunities for personal development of every individual in an open society. But it is not enough to build on the negotiating abilities of the potentially affected alone because only specialists can anticipate the complex impacts of dams. Therefore participation presupposes that the mediation process contains a substantial informative component.

Relying solely on a mediation process is also not sufficient in providing for social impacts. There is no generally recognised method to determine the value of 'goods' in a subsistence economy. Without objective criteria, the moral demands on both sides are extremely high. Strategically-motivated behaviour will then not be prevented even if all participants agree readily that the subjective standard of living of people affected by a dam should be improved or at least maintained.

Mediation processes make sense only if agreements are observed. According to the WCD analyses, lack of compliance with agreements is the main cause of the negative social impacts of dams. In the case of dam projects cofinanced by international donors, disbursements of funding instalments could depend upon independent evaluations that confined compliance. Ensuring compliance is much more difficult in the case of projects financed by the private sector. Because there is no independent institution that could assume the role of arbitrator, it must be in the business world's own interests to act responsibly in ecological and social terms. To be credible, it must provide transparency and independent certifiers.

Due to the opposing interests involved, no-one should expect reaching consensus to be easy. But the example set by the WCD is not the only reason for hope. Taking a closer look at it, the model offers significant advantages for all participants. Partner countries and development organisations wish to continue to use the potential for development which dams will also offer in the future. The private sector will also continue to build and operate dams, and for that they need planning certainly. The advantages for NGOs and the people affected are also obvious.

21

Water Facts and Findings on Large Dams

Water Facts

Today, around 3800 km^3 of fresh water is withdrawn annually from the world's lakes, rivers and aquifers. This is twice the volume extracted 50 years algo. World population has passed 6 billion. Projections say that it will reach a peak of between 7.3 billion and 10.7 billion around 2050 before total population begins to stabilise or fall.

50 litres per person per day (or just over 18.25 m^3 a year) covers basic human water requirements for drinking, sanitation, bathing and food preparation. In 1990, over a billion people ahead access to less than 50 litres of water a day. Agriculture accounts for about 67% of withdrawals, industry uses 19% and municipal and domestic uses account for 9%.

One third of the countries in water stressed regions of the world are expected to face severe water shortages this century. By 2025 there will be approximately 6.5 times as many people—a total of 3.5 billion living in water-stressed countries. By the end of the 20th century, there were over 45,000 large dams in over 150 countries. The average large dam today is about 35 years old. Since average construction periods generally range from 5 to 10 years, this indicates a worldwide annual average of some 160 to 320 new large dams per year.

During the 1990s, an estimated $32-46 billion was spent annually on large dams, four-fifths of it in developing countries. Of the $22-31 billion invested in dams each year in developing countries, about four-fifths was financed directly by the public sector. About one-fifth of the world's agricultural land is irrigated, and irrigated agriculture accounts for about 40% of the world's agricultural production.

Half the world's large dams were built exclusively or primarily for irrigation, and an estimated 30 to 40% of the 271 million hectares of irrigated lands worldwide rely on dams. Dams are estimated to contribute to 12-16% of world food production. Hydropower currently provides 19% of the world total electricity supply, and is used in over 150 countries with 24 of these countries depending on it for 90% of their supply.

Floods affected the lives on average, of 65 million people between 1972 and 1996, more than any other type of disaster, including war, drought and famine. There are 261 water sheets that cross the political boundaries two are more countries. A number of key international rivers lack a basin-wide agreement that defines a process for establishing equitable water use between riparian States.

Cost Effectiveness

Cost performance data confirms that large dam projects often incur substantial capital cost overruns. The average overrun was half again as much as the projected cost. The bulk of hydropower projects have delivered power within a close range of pre-project targets but with an overall tendency to fall short of targets.

At current rates, water fees are rarely sufficient to recover both capital and recurrent costs for water supply systems in many developing countries. Growing concern over the cost and effectiveness of large dams and related structural measures as long-term responses to floods has led to support for integrated flood management as opposed to flood control.

Multi-purpose schemes are inherently more complex, and many experience operational conflicts that contribute to under-performance on financial and economic targets. Substantive evaluations of project performance are few in number, narrow in scope, and poorly integrated across impact categories and scales.

Ecological Costs

Dams, inter basin transfers, and water withdrawals for irrigation have fragmented 60% of the world's rivers. As a physical barrier the dam disrupts the movement in upstream and downstream species composition and even species loss. In Africa, the changed hydrological regime of rivers has adversely affected floodplain agriculture, fisheries, pasture and forests that constituted the organising element of community livelihood and culture.

Problems may be magnified as more large dams are added to a river system, resulting in a n increased and cumulative loss of natural resources, habitat quality, environmental sustainability and ecosystem integrity. Good site selection, such as not building large dams on the main-stem of a river system, and better dam design also played significant roles in avoiding or minimising impacts. The economic appraisal techniques such as risk and distributional analysis were still mandated for only 20% of large dam projects even in the 1990s.

Social Costs

At the planning and design stage, an important social impact is the delay between he decision to build a dam and the onset of construction. This can result in communities living for decades starved of development and welfare investments.

The overall global level of physical displacement could range from 40 to 80 million. In India and China together, large dams could have displaced between 26-58 million people between 1950 and 1990. Little or no meaningful participation of affected people in the planning and implementation of dam projects—including resettlement and rehabilitation has taken place.

Empowering people, particularly the economically and socially marginalised by respecting their rights and ensuring that resettlement with development becomes a process governed by negotiated agreements is critical to positive resettlement and rehabilitation.

Poor accounting in economic terms for the social and environmental costs and benefits of large dams implies that the rue economic efficiency and profitability of these schemes remains largely unknown.

The direct adverse impacts of dams have fallen disproportionately on rural dwellers, subsistence farmers, indigenous people, ethnic minorities, and women. Where costs and benefits accrue to different groups, the standard procedures for adding up and discounting the expected costs and benefits do not provide an appropriate measure of changes in social welfare.

Financing

Almost 2 billion people, both urban and rural poor, have no access to electricity at all. Most efficiency measures and technologies are cost effective at today's electricity prices and the use of full environmental and social costing of electricity supply options makes them even more so. Among advanced technologies in research and development, micro turbines and fuel cell show the greatest near and mid-term promise.

Total financing for large dams from multi—lateral and bi-lateral development banks comes to more than $4 billion annually at the peak of lending during 1975-84. Although the proportion of investment in dams directly financed by bi-laterals and multilateral was perhaps less than 15%. The total investment in dams by the multilaterals and bilaterals since 1950 is approximately $125 billion.

22

Trading Towards Peace

The reason why trade has such a vital part to play in building peace is because it means lowering barriers—not only to goods and services but among nations and nations and peoples. The elimination of barriers creates interdependence and interdependence creates solidarity. The history of the last fifty years has shown us all the undeniable benefits of lowering trade barriers and opening economies.

Clearly every region has its own characteristics, and it would be wrong to imagine that the same blueprint can apply everywhere and in the same way. Any region which was for thousands of years at the crosswords of world trade should regain its place in the centre, because doing so will help build peace as well as prosperity. This is why the numerous applications for accession to the WTO from various countries are so significant. The first is through regionalism. There are several efforts at regional trade and economic initiatives among countries, and that such initiatives will be encouraged to reduce positive results. Regional initiatives are important because they can help countries at a comparable level of development to move relatively quickly in opening their economies and in deepening their interdependence.

However, the rapid advance of global economic integration means that while regional initiatives remain important, they are not sufficient by themselves to address successfully the new perspectives of the international economy. That is why there is a need for second track, which is the rule-based multilateral system.

And that is why the multilateral system is of fundamental importance to the economic prosperity of any region.

As the first major international institution to be created in the post-Cold War era, the WTO offers a promise of the kind of global economic architecture which need in the coming decades. Its culture is firmly rooted in the tradition of consensus-building and coopeation among sovereign countries. And the WTO embodies rights and obligations negotiated by consensus, approved and ratified by each government and each parliament, and they are enforceable, not through the crude exercise of economic power, but through the rule of law. The alternative would be a power-based system—who would want to chose this option?

But most importantly the WTO is an organisation which brings all countries—from all corners of the world and from all levels of development—together as equals. There is no weighted voting, no exclusive clubs, no inner and outer circles. Developing countries representing 80% of constituency sit as equals with industrialized countries to write the rules of a shared trading system.

This new unity of developing and developed countries inside a single system will be credited as the greatest achievement of the multilateral system. But this unity is still fragile: we cannot allow it to be broken: This is why, in preparing the agenda of the first Ministerial meeting in Singapore, have recognized the particularly difficult task facing developing countries in implementing the Uruguay Round Commitments. They have also acknowledged the challenges they face in contemplating the necessary work programme.

The integration of developing countries as equal partners in the multilateral system is one of the most important challenges in shaping the economic order of the 21st century. This is a shared responsibility of developed and developing countries alike. There is no rational alternative to this objective. The evolution of the global economy makes that clear.

Now there is a need to work together as equal partners to ensure the full integration, and all other developing and transition economies, into the global economy and the rule-based multilateral trading system. In conjunction with this there is a need to encourage, notably with growth of regional economic cooperation. The alternative is a vicious circle where economic isolation feeds greater political instability which in turn leads to greater economic isolation. The road to a lasting peace in the world begins, not ends, with economic irritegration and Interdependence. Taking this message to heart will help build a future where it is goods, services, and investment that cross borders—not missiles and soldiers.

23

Development: *The Third Way*

While great claims are being made for the increasingly more efficient and effective technologies perfected to serve development of the people in this scientific age, huge problems are threatening the globe. The problems are mass poverty and hunger, underdevelopment, waste, unemployment, resource scarcity, environmental destruction and armed conflict.

In finding answers to the prevailing problems we must be clear about the meaning and purpose of development. The first glaring mistake made is that development is interpreted as development of the economy and not as the total development of society. When economic development is made the supreme goal, most of the other vital aspects get ignored, namely, development of the political system, community, social cohesion, the ecology, culture and values, development and stability go hand in hand while poverty and chaos constitute the antithetical twin.

Appropriate Development

The key elements in the conception of appropriate development consist of: first, aiming at sufficiently comfortable material living standards and not affluent standards of the rich as in prosperous nations. Second, development must not be confused with GNP growth. Mere increase of economic activity must not be pursued exclusively at the cost of articles that are urgently needed by the poor majority to maintain them at a reasonable level of material living. Third, in the villages, we must produce articles as are needed by the villagers. Fourth grassroots and participatory development is essential so that the local people identify and solve their local problems. Fifth, instead of capital and energy intensive high technology, use labour-intensive technology, Instead of heavy indistrialisation, promote medium scale industries and technologies. And, sixth, instead of preoccupation with a high GNP growth rate, focus on the development of communities and of rural bodies and take care to conserve the local ecosystems. The main purpose should be to meet their primary needs of ordinary people and promotion of their productive resources such as land.

In developing countries like India where billions of poor people remain condemned by conventional economic development strategies and theories, it is vital to introduce appropriate development measures to remove deprivation and ensure the necessity of modest living standards.

The world has witnessed the operation of the two systems namely, the capitalist and the socialist one that have obtained in different countries. Although both the systems have underlined the welfare of all as the basic goal, both have left a legacy of waste, hunger and gross human inequality. Some 1000 million people do not get enough to eat including some 20 million in the USA.

Third World Way of Development

The iniquitous situation in the present day world has sparked off fierce controversies among the conventional economists and the new radical economists who champion a third way, as the alternative way to serve the primary goal of all humanity to have sufficient means to lead a comfortable peaceful life.

In order to achieve prosperity, conventional economists have emphasized the production of bigger cake on the assumption that everyone will get a slice of it. They also argue that a "tide will lift all the boats". Both these assumptions have proved false in that the poor have neither the slice of cake nor has their boat been lifted. Third way system lays stress on highly localized, less cash-reliant and simply structured set-up. It should not be dependent on transport of goods, but concentrate on more local production to meet local needs with a role for barter and free exchange. He urges a radical re-think of conventional economics.

Is this Stepping Backwards?

The most common criticism levelled against the Third Way is that it will arrest the progress made hitherto and that it might mean a return to a 'primitive' way of life. There should be no fear on this score because the Third Way aims at the reduction in the use of resources and therefore, of excessive production and consumption. It does not in any sense mean stepping backwards to a lower level of the quality of life. Nor is the alternative way intended to destroy capitalism or socialism. The conception of the alternate way is to promote economic growth compatible with capitalism and socialism. The ground idea is to promote selflessness, mutual concern and social responsibility. This will replace selfish, competitive and avaricious attitudes as have developed in the conventional economic order of today.

NGO's Resolution at the Rio Conference

That there is increasing awareness of the threat posed by the growing power of multinational corproations was articulated by the international NGO forum in its Declaration resolved on 12 June 1992 at the UN Conference of Environment and Development in Rio de Janeiro. The declaration states that "the Bretton Woods institutions have served the major instruments by which the destruction policies have been imposed on the world" and calls upon "the world's people to protect their economic, social, cultural and environmental interests against the growing power of transnational capital". The declaration further avers "we recognize the central place of spiritual values and spiritual development... and values of simplicity, love, peace, and reverence for life.

After the failure of the socialist system over four decades to achieve prosperity for all, the Indian Government switched over to the global market economy and is steaming ahead with added liberalisation measures to attract foreign investment and the multinational corproations (MNCs). Some adverse effects of this are already visible: for example, majority financial equity granted to MNCs and the emergence of foreign subsidiaries with cent per cent financial equity; the introduction of pizza and Kentucky Fried Chicken which has been detested by the people in Karnataka. The farmers have also revolted because their rights to produce and sell seeds have been wrested by foreign MNCs who have acquired patent rights over certain Indian crop seeds. In this scenario, the third Way has much to commend itself to the Government. The Third Way has the air of the Gandhian model of economy and production which emphasizes production by people for their own needs and preference for small and medium sized industry. The same paradigm was championed by the renowned economist Schumachar when he said "Small is beautiful". India should take good care against the present-day headlong drive for the entry of foreign capital and foreign heavy industries.

24

A New World Order for Whom?

"Four holocausts" humanity has produced are breeding the seeds of our own destruction: war and militarisation, human oppression, economic destitution and environmental destruction. The "new world orders" on offer can satisfy only the minority of the world's rich and will ultimately only exacerbate these four trends towards global annihilation. But there is also hope in the "grassroots world order" leading to the civil society, democratisation and social mobilisation as the only way for the planet to survive.

As we approach the end of the 20th century and a new millenium, humanity is faced with four conditions of its own making, so serious in terms of their present destruction of life and risks for the future that they warrant a description as "four holocausts".

The first holocaust is that of war and militarisation. After the Gulf War it is clear that, far from preparing the way for world peace, that conflict has unleashed a new global arms race in the weapons whose brutal effectiveness was so clearly demonstrated in Iraq. The second holocaust is that of human oppression, the violent denial by governments of the basic personal, civil, political and economic rights of their citizens, which routinely persist in a majority of countries of the world. The third holocaust is that of economic destitution, the mass poverty of a fifth of the world's population, leading to endemic malnutrition, disease and death, not least among children. And the fourth holocaust is that of environmental destruction, which is gradually or not so gradually rendering the planet uninhabitable, as witnessed by the growing millions of environmental refugees whose bankrupt ecosystems can no longer support them.

None of these circumstances is entirely new to our age, of course, war, repression, destitution and ecological degradation have often been part of the human condition. What is new about the current situation is its global nature. All humanity, the whole earth, is now at risk. And it is all humanity which must be party to a response, if it is to be successful.

Against this threatening background, several new developments stand out. First, is the collapse of communism, taking out of the bounds of credibility socialism's millenarian dream of abolishing the market and inevitably replacing capitalism through the onward march of history. Second, there are the twin trends of globalisation and interdependence: globalisation especially of the economy, interdependence especially through environmental impacts. This is the context for any discussion of a "new world order".

The New World Orders

There are, broadly, three kinds of new world orders currently on offer. The real world is almost certainly going to be mixture of all three, but the balance between them will be crucial in deciding whether we will successfully manage to face, and overcome, the holocausts raging among us.

The first kind of new world order may be called the "neoliberal". Its most important component is the untrammelled operation of what we would call the global "free market". At once we must qualify this terminology by noting that the freedom bestowed on someone by the market is in direct proportion to the amount of property owned by that person within it. In a free market, those who own the means of production are free to produce what, when and where they want, and largely to determine the conditions of production. Those who own the means of consumption can similarly scour the world for products to satisfy their wants. The extent to which this "freedom" is far from universal is shown by the fact that, within regard to consumption some 23 per cent of the world's population control 85 per cent of the income which is consumptions prerequisite and ownership of the means of production is more concentrated still. The neoliberal world order thus represents a good deal for perhaps a quarter of the world's population, but has precious little to offer the rest.

A Global Order Framed by International Institutions

The second kind of new world order may be termed the "social democratic" and is roughtly that advocated in the 1970's by the proponents of a New International Economic Order. These two new world orders clearly different but they also share several characteristics which seem to be more significant than their differences. First, they are explicitly western-oriented and homogenizing. They view the world through the eyes of western science and western culture simultaneously devaluating the knowledge and accumulated wisdom of the great majority of human kind. The paradigm society, towards which all others are supposed to be developing or aspiring to develop, is that of the United States.

Second, both these world orders are economistic. Human progress and development to them means economic developments, still usually measured by the level and growth of GNP per person. No social or cultural tradition or aspiration is allowed to stand in the way of this "development". Third, both world views envisage top-down decision-making for administration and control. For the neoliberals the dominant influence is exercised by the owners and managers of transnational capital. For the social democrats their influence is balanced by the interventions of international and national bureaucrats. Neither world order places great store on consultation with, let alone decision-making by, ordinary people in their communities.

In contrast to these two new world orders, it is possible to posit a third, here called the grassroots new world order, which takes as its principal focus neither the market nor the state (national or international), but civil society, the networks of family, community and voluntary association acting for social reproduction, reconstruction or reform. This new world order has characteristics diametrically opposed to those shared by the first two discussed. Its impulse derives explicitly from the bottom up, drawing on the capability and creativity of those united by shared values and interests, at the local level or in wider networks. Their world-view is one of cultural diversity, of one world comprised of many different villages rather than a homogeneous global village modelled on the US. They perceive human development to be holistic, with the economic dimension integrated with, or embedded in, a broader social, ethical and ecological reality. And they proceed from an ethical basis that strives for ecological sustainability, social justice in distribution and broad participation is cultural, political and economic life.

Looking to the Grassroots World Order

After this thumbnail sketch of these three views of different dominant global processes, one can ask which of them or, more realistically, what balance between them, will be best able to put an end to the four holocausts tormenting humanity. There is only one convincing answer: the dominant thrust must be towards the grassroots new world order. There are several reasons for this. Most obviously, it is indisputable that it is the forces of the market and the state that have not only failed to douse, but have actually fanned the flames of all four holocausts. It is states that go to war and waste the commonwealth on weaponry. It is states that are responsible for the great majority of violence and repression against ordinary people. It is states, often supported by multilateral governmental organisations such as the World Bank and IMF, that have the so called Third World intervened massively in the subsistence, largely nonmarket economies of he people, and redistributed their resources, redefining their very rights to property, in favour of industrialisation and market exchange. But these enhanced markets have then spectacularly failed to provide alternative subsistence for those dispossessed, leaving them by the million impoverished, marginalized and destitute. Moreover, this process has set in train two great engines of environmental destruction: industrialisation itself, with its toxic pollution, soil erosion, water and ozone depletion and climate destabilisation; and the depredations of the rural dispossessed, forced into forests or onto marginal lands, deforesting, making deserts, extinguishing species and multiplying in numbers of their desperate efforts to stay alive.

Civil Society Mobilizing for Human Survival

In contrast, it is civil society that has mobilized explicitly against the four holocausts. The great social movements of our time are those for peace and human rights, for justice and development, and for environmental conservation. It is independent, non-violent associations of civil society that have sought explicitly to address these issues, meeting at best indifference from organisations of the market and the state, at worst outright hostility.

This is not at all to say that the market and state are irredeemable, or that they have no role in combating the four holocausts of destruction. On the contrary, they each have a vital contribution to make but, it order to make it, each must first be transformed. The market failures caused by great concentrations of wealth and power, ubiquitous externalities, the tyranny of small decisions and positional goods can only be resolved by determined and democratic state action. But most governments are not democratic. On the contrary most are unrepresentative and self-serving, many are vicious and corrupt. And the only force that can democratize them is that of civil mobilisation and organisation.

Viewing the immense power of today's concentrations of wealth, and the remoteness of most governments from their people, one may feel despair at the prospect of civil society being able to harness these forces to the common good. And indeed there is no certainty that they will be thus harnessed. The four holocausts may simply run their awful course. But since 1989, at least, there is proof positive in the peaceful revolutions in Eastern Europe and the Soviet Union, that civil society can overturn seemingly omnipotent despotic structures. And all over the world the various movements for peace, justice and the environment are organizing for human survival. The stakes have never been so high and the outcome is uncertain; but there are legitimate, and inspiring, grounds for hope.

25

State Trading Enterprises: *Existence of Monopolies is No Longer Justified*

Agricultural state trading enterprises (STEs), used by some countries to control imports and encourage exports for non-commercial reasons, no longer have a place in global agriculture. STEs not only diminish benefits that other exporters expect in third-country markets, but they may create additional costs for producers, prompt predatory pricing practices that drive other exporters out of particular markets, and keep more producers in business and more land in production than would otherwise be the case.

The new disciplines on agricultural trade established in the Uruguay Round and the globalisation of international agricultural trade raise important questions about the role of state trading enterprises. Traditional reasons for maintaining STEs have included controlling imports, encouraging exports for non-commercial reasons (such as obtaining foreign exchange or removing surplus production), or establishing emergency food stockpiles.

However, rules prohibiting the maintenance of nontariff barriers through STEs and disciplines on export subsidies have eliminated most of their traditional purposes. As a consequence, agricultural STEs are a concern among many World Trade Organisation (WTO) members because of their potential to distort trade. Much of the concern arises from the substantial market power wielded by monopoly STE exporters and importers, commonly referred to as single-desk sellers and buyers. Some of the common characteristics of single-desk sellers and buyers are described here, along with some of the potential trade distortions that may result from the operation of the single-desk system.

Single-Desk Sellers

Single-desk sellers have common characteristics that may give them advantages in international trade and may lead to trade distortions. These include a lack of price transparency; government financial backing that may insulate them from the financial risks normally faced by other exporters; an ability to control procurement costs by maintaining monopsony control over purchases for domestic and export sales; an ability to "price discriminate" using cross-subsidisation, either between the domestic and export markets or between different buyers; and the ability to insulate produccers from market prices through price-pooling schemes. These characteristics and the distortions that they cause may diminish benefits that other exporters expect in third-country markets. Besides their potential to distort trade, single-desk sellers may create additional costs for producers or allocate inefficiencies caused by production drive by non-market price signals.

Monopoly authority and the lack of transparency in export pricing may provide single-desk sellers with greater pricing flexibility relative to private traders. In the private export trade, commodity prices, which are in effect "replacement values" for exported products, are quoted daily on various market exchanges. Private exporters have no choice but to buy their export supplies at a given market price, which is widely known in the trade and to governments. Single-desk sellers, in contrast, and not required to reveal their transaction prices. This may put them in a position to disguise procurement costs and subsequent export prices, particularly when export sales are subsidized through direct or indirect government subsidies.

Many single-desk sellers benefit from the financial backing of the Central Government, either through direct subsidies or from government guarantees. Because single-desk sellers are quasi-governmental entities or direct government agencies, their operational losses, which generally have been caused by pooling account deficits, are in most cases reimbursed by the federal government. The actual intervention by the government, or the functional equivalent afford through the assurance of government intervention, shields producers from risk and encourages production because producers can rely on support when faced with reduced revenue from declining prices. This encourages higher levels of production than otherwise would occur.

Single-desk sellers are monopsony buyers for export and frequently monopolists for re-sales in the domestic market. As such, they can force producers to accept lower prices than might otherwise be possible under more competitive conditions. This is particularly important when a country exports a substantial share of total production. Producers, who frequently have no alternative crops to cultivate for geographic reasons, have no alternative but to sell to the single-desk exporter and take whatever price is offered, giving the single-desk seller wide flexibility in export pricing. Additionally, this control leaves open the opportunity for the single-desk seller to reduce, delay, or otherwise manipulate the price it pays producers to acquire supplies. The pricing power may be behind a host of many other practices that can lead to trade distortions, including price discrimination.

In world markets, where prices are normally outside the control of sellers in a particularly country, the ability to price discriminate may represent a significant advantage for a single-desk seller. It may also lead to higher levels of imports into particular WTO member countries than world occur under perfectly competitive conditions. Price discrimination occurs when a single-desk seller can differentiate its sales prices for comparable quality commodities between different destinations according to a buyer's ability to pay. The ability to discriminate allows a single-desk seller to maximize returns among a range of purchasers with different price elasticities by lowering prices to certain buyers without affecting its higher sales price in premium markets. Since single-desk sellers control their procurement costs, they have more power to raise and lower prices across different markets.

If single-desk sellers are obliged to purchase all domestic production, the ability to price discriminate allows then to lower costs to whatever level is necessary to unload the product in foreign markets. Similarly, when single-desk sellers are driven by government policy objectives, such as maximizing production or exports rather than profits, sales in high-price markets can underwrite the sale of surplus products at uneconomical prices. Additionally, price discrimination encourages the use of predatory pricing practices, whereby a monopoly seller lowers its prices to drive other exporters out of a particular market. If successful, the single-desk seller can raise prices once the competition has been eliminated.

Price-pooling arrangements that are operated by single-desk sellers are intended to equalize payments to producers while minimizing the risk inherent in marketing their products. Under an pooling system, farmers deliver their product to a pool controlled by the single-desk seller in return for a initial payment. At the end of a marketing year, the single-desk seller tallies its total sales revenues and deducts marketing and other operational costs. The net revenue is then distributed to the producers. Under this system, each farmer, in effect, receives a blended price based on all sales for the year . Diversifying sales reduces the risk borne by producers, but it also leaves all export pricing decisions to the single-desk seller, which may set prices based on a range of government policy objectives. Although pooling helps reduce market risk for producers by acting to stabilize prices received during the marketing year, costs are inherent in the pooling system. For example, producers of higher-quality products, those that have achieved marketing efficiencies, or those that deliver products to the pool during a period of higher world prices are effectively penalized because they may receive a blended price derived from a lower-quality grade or from revenue generated by lower-priced sales. As a consequence, wealth is transferred from high-quality producers to lower-quality producers, which may keep more producers in business and more land in production than otherwise would be the case.

Single-desk Buyers

Single-desk buyers may be able to restrict or otherwise distort trade in several ways—lack of transparency, interference with end-users, enforcement of burdensome requirements on imported products, and procurement of emergency stockpiles. These and other purchasing and marketing practices may raise domestic prices and impair market access opportunities for exporters. Monopoly control over imports and the resulting market power of single-desk buyers may allow them to restrict access for imported products based on government-determined criteria, not on commercial considerations. This decision can be made without regard to prevailing world market conditions or domestic demand considerations. Ultimately, this control gives the single-desk buyer the flexibility to support internal prices and to otherwise regulate demand for imports.

Single-desk buyers generally provide insufficient transparency regarding their purchases and sells. Information on import pricing, resale pricing, requested grades and quality, and purchase quantities are not available to traders or the public. Lack of this information makes it difficult for exporters and domestic end-users to do business and may allow the single-desk buyer to disguise trade restrictions.

State control of marketing and distribution may interfere with end-user purchasing decisions—in contrast to direct contact between exporters and end-users, which allows the specification of grade and quality and leads to increased value of imported products to the end-user. This benefits end-users and consumers, but it can also benefit exporters who develop marketing relationships and receive higher prices by dealing with end-users who value the grade and quality of their products. However, when these decisions must go through single-desk importers, the importer can enforce other government policy objectives, such as discouraging imports of competitive grades and qualities or "luxury" imports, that restrict imports.

Single-desk buyers may be empowered to enforce burdensome requirements on imported products. Marketing control including control of internal marketing and distribution of imports, also gives the single-desk seller the ability to direct imports of inferior quality products that may be less competitive than domestically produced products. Retail pricing, promotion, and distribution of imported products are often controlled by the single-desk buyer. This may interfere with consumer preferences and efficient resource allocation, especially when marketing strategy is formulated by a state-controlled entity rather than a private firm that is subject to market competition.

26

Developing Countries and the Uruguay Round: *An Evaluation and Prospects for the Future*

The Uruguay Round was the most ambitious trade negotiation in history. It covered a wide variety of subjects relating to trade in goods; it brought under the aegis of multilateral disciplines two new sectors—agriculture and textiles—which had previously been exempt from such disciplines; it established new rules for services and intellectual property; and it set up a new World Trade Organisation (WTO) charged with supervising the results of the Round and continuing negotiations on all trade-related questions.

This article focuses on key issues of interest to developing countries. They are: (a) market access for developing country exports; (b) new restrictions on trade and industrial policy formulation in developing countries; (c) the effectiveness of the new safeguards and antidumping mechanisms in deterring protectionism; (d) the protection of intellectual property rights; (e) services; (f) the status of the principle of special and differential (S&D) treatment; and (g) institutional reforms and the creation of the WTO. An evaluation of the Round from the point of view of developing countries must necessarily attempt to weigh all of these elements.

The results of the Uruguay Round do not represent a good deal for developing countries. As regards improved market access for developing country exports, tariffs on products of interest to developing countries have been cut, but they will remain at higher levels than those applied to products traded mainly among developed countries; moreover, tariff escalation will be reduced but not significantly, The Round will being about only marginal improvements in market access in the crucial areas of agriculture and textiles. Developing countries should continue to fight for the removal of tariffs on those goods that are of export interest to them and for the elimination of tariff escalation.

Market access will also depend on the abolition of grey area measures, their replacement by transparent and clearly temporary safeguard provisions, and the disciplining of antidumping practices. The new safeguards mechanism agreed to in the Round is due to replace grey area measures. However, the agreement legitimizes quantitative restrictions (QRS) directed at individual exporters, albeit with fairly stringent limitations as to duration and proof of injury procedures. Moreover, it remains to be seen in practice whether importers will resort to safeguards or will prefer the route of antidumping measures, which will remain easier to apply. Indeed, the antidumping agreement can be considered the major loophole of the Final Act and may well lead to a recrudescence of protectionism in both developed and-by imitation- developing countries.

The single most important achievement of the Uruguay Round was the setting up under the aegis of the WTO of an integrated and strengthened dispute settlement mechanism. While cross retaliation has been legitimized as a last resort, defendants will no longer be able to veto panel decisions that go against them. However, it is not yet clear to what extent the new dispute settlement mechanism will succeed in deterring major importers from having recourse to unilateral measures (such as those taken by the United States under the cover of Section 301 of the 1984 Trade Act).

As a result of the Round, there has been a significant upward harmonisation of trade and industrialisation policy disciplines towards the standards prevailing in developed countries. Henceforth, developing countries will face considerably more stringent restrictions in these areas, and their access to foreign technology will become more uncertain and costly. The Round has also resulted in a significant erosion in the international consensus in favour of special and differential (S & D) treatment for developing countries in the international trading system.

As the accords are implemented, developing countries will experience balance-of-payments difficulties. There will be a need to provide developing countries with greater International Monetary Found (IMF) financing during the transition to the new disciplines, many of which will have adverse repercussions on the balance of payments of developing countries. Some of the agreements with balance-of-payments implications for developing countries are the adoption and enforcement of stricter intellectual property legislation, the agreement on agriculture, and the restrictions, on the use of trade measures to protect the balance of payments.

The Final Act calls for Cooperation between the WTO the World Bank and the IMF. In the long term, the main area of cooperation ought to be ensuring the consistency of international policies in the areas of trade, money and finance in order to ensure high rates of growth in the world economy and in developing countries in particular. It is especially important that such cooperation does not become an additional source of pressure on developing countries or restrict their degree of freedom in policy formulation and implementation.

In future trade negotiations, developing countries should emphasize improvements in the S & D principle, which should be made contractual in all of its dimensions. As a quid proquo, developing countries should be ready to accept internationally agreed and binding criteria for graduation from the special and differential treatment category. Thus, belonging to the category of "developing" would no longer be a matter of self-election. Likewise, developed countries would no longer be able to graduate countries at their own discretion. Countries classified as developing would enjoy access to a truly generlized and universal GSP and temporary derogation from some of the disciplines imposed on developed countries. Those derogations would apply to all areas of the agreement. The criteria used for graduation ought to include, besides per capita GDP, indicators of the level of industrial development. In the short term, the S & D principle can be usefully applied, in the process of "tariffication" of NTBs called for in the agreement on agriculture, by giving developing countries access to developed country markets at lower bound tariff rates than those applicable to developed country exporters.

The agreement on safeguards has problematic aspects. Close monitoring will be required so as to prevent the major trading partners—and, perhaps, by imitation, some developing countries themselves—from using the loopholes in the agreement (particularly the right to use QRs and the "quota modulation" provision) to reintroduce grey area measures, now under the legal cover of the safeguards agreement. The addition of a clause calling for payment of financial compensation to parties affected by quantitative safeguards when they exceed a certain maximum duration would deter countries from abusing the system. To be sure, the Uruguay Round cannot be considered to have settled the debate on this issue.

The Uruguay Round has given legal sanction to the new protectionism in the form of very unsatisfactory antidumping rules. This is an area that will undoubtedly continue to figure prominently on the agenda of future international trade negotiations. As a minimum, all the facts presented to national panels in antidumping cases should be subjected to review by the Dispute Settlement Board. The use of reconstructed values in determining the existence of dumping and calculating dumping margins should be eliminated altogether. The antidumping mechanism would be improved if a clear distinction were made between price discrimination (Which ought to be legal) and predatory printing. The optimal solution would be to eliminate antidumping completely and to include the issue of predatory pricing within the framework of competition policy.

Harmonizatin of competion policy has often been mentioned as a major item for the Post-Uruguary Round trade agenda. Two issues of particular interest to developing countries in this area relate to investment measures and intellectual property. Particular TRIMs—such as export performance, local content, and trade-balancing requirements were seen in the Uruguay Round mainly as trade distortions, although they are also means of offsetting the restrictive business practices of transnational corporations. These practices should be subsumed under efforts to harmonize international competition policies. Similarly, many intellectual property issues impinge directly on competition policy. Impediments to "parallell" imports of patented goods can give rise to questions of competition. A major competition policy issue is the question of the scope and length of patent protection.

Much remains to be done in the area of trade in services. Developing countries ought to press for greater liberalisation of the temporary movement of skilled labour and labour working in the employment of services companies. The initial offers on services in the framework of the General Agreement on Trade in Services (GATS) largely exclude this code of delivery of services to foreign markets, a mode of critical interest to developing countries. Great caution and selectivity needs to be exercised with regard to the liberalisation of financial services; in this respect, the GATs gives developing countries the legal instrument to follow a gradual and selective approach. However, they will have to be prepared to resists bilateral pressures from sone of their developed country partners to liberalize their financial services sector too rapidly.

Incorporation into the WTO implies a major domestic challenge for most developing countries. They will have to make efforts to change and adapt domestic legislation in a large number of new areas, including services, intellectual property, and several areas of trade policy that have received little attention in the past (e.g. safeguards, subsidies, and antidumping). The enforcement and administrative capacities of national institutions will have to be built up.

The WTO has been given a mandate to include in future negotiations any trade-related subject. The issues of environment and labour standards seem to be first in line. It will not be an easy matter to harmonize policies in theses areas.

The reason is that harmonisation can be expected to take the form of aligning policies on developed country standards. It would be naive to pretend that the demands of environmental groups and labour unions on these matters can simply be ignored. Therefore, the challenge ahead is to participate constructively in drafting multilateral rules which expand or preserve access to markets and preclude punitive unilateral action, while taking into consideration environmental and labour concerns.

27

The WTO and the Developing Countries

The special status of developing countries in the GATT will continue to receive recognition in the WTO. The preamble of the Agreement Establishing the WTO states that "there is a need for positive efforts designed to ensure that developing countries, and especially the least developed among them, secure a share in the growth of international trade commensurate with the needs of their economic development". In addition to retaining the provision that concerned developing countries in GATT 1947, the new agreement generally contain provisions for developing counties and least-developed countries, often consisting of longer transition periods for the full implementation of some obligations and various exemptions from obligations, particularly for the latter group of countries. Also, in some instances, the exports of developing countries benefit from a better treatment with respect to measures taken by other WTO Members. Technical assistance is to be provided to developing countries to assist them in assuming their obligations and more effectively realizing the benefits of the multilateral trading system.

Least-developed countries are singled out in the Final Act as requiring special attention. This is reflected in the agreements through a number of provisions which provide the most favourable treatment for this group in terms of rights as well as lower levels of obligations. In addition, the Decision on Measures in Favour of Least-Developed Countries, makes provision for measures of special assistance, including technical assistance "in the development, strengthening and diversification of their production and export bases including those of services, as well as in trade promotion, to enable them to maximize the benefits from liberalized access to markets". As part of its functions, the Committee on Trade and Development (a subsidiary body of the General Council) will periodically review the special provisions in favour of least-developed countries and report to the General Council of the WTO for appropriate action.

The Declaration on the Contribution of the WTO to Achieving Greater Coherence in Global Economic Policy making identifies the need for strengthening the relationship between the activities of the WTO, the International Monetary Fund (IMF) and the World Bank as a way of ensuring greater coherence in global economic policy-making.

Market Access

Industrial Products: For developed countries, the main features of their market access commitments in industrial products include the expansion of bindings to cover 99 per cent of imports; the expansion of duty free access from 30 to 44 per cent of total imports; and the reduction of the trade-weighted average tariff by 40 per cent (i. e. from the per-Uruguay Round level of 6.2 per cent to the post-Uruguay Round level of 3.7 per cent). With respect to tariff reductions on individual product categories, developed countries will reduce tariffs by substantially above-average amounts (60 per cent or more) in three categories—wood, pulp, paper and furniture; metals; and non-electric machinery and reduce tariffs by less than the 40 per cent overall reduction in four categories—fish and fish products; textiles and clothing; leather, rubber, footwear; and transport equipment.

In terms of exports from developing to developed country markets, the total reduction in the average tariff of developed countries is 37 per cent. Below average tariff reductions, and above-average levels of tariffs apply to labour-intensive manufacturers (textiles and clothing, leather goods) and certain processed primary products (fish products) that have been—and continue to be—regarded as "sensitive".

Developed countries constitute the most important merchandise exports market for developing countries (62 per cent in 1992). In part, this is because the developed countries account for the bulk of global income and expenditures. At the same time, market access opportunities for developing countries in each other's markets have long been affected by the protection in their own markets. In many instances, the level of protection is quite high, because important protection, ultimately, acts as a tax on exports as well, protection in developing countries also hinders the integration of developing countries also hinders the integration of developing economies, not just with each other, but with the larger global trading system.

The reductions in bound tariffs which the new commitments of developing economies represent are difficult to assess for several reasons. The first is that comprehensive information on base (1986) tariffs is unavailable in many cases as a result of the low level of bindings among developing countries. In these cases, the post-Uruguay Round average bound tariff usually involves a decrease in the ceiling bindings applied to items already found, combined with ceiling bindings above currently applied rates for previously unbound items. Another reason is that, where developing economies had bound all or a significant portion of tariffs prior to the end of the Round, the Uruguay Round tariff commitments often reflect a decline in ceiling rates (rather than applied rates).

At the same time, current tariff levels already reflect the often substantial reductions undertaken autonomously in the course of the Round. Though many developing countries may not be required to introduce further cuts, previous liberalisation has been at least partly locked in through new commitments on bindings. Ceiling bindings are considered to be so important that countries which agree to bind previously unbound tariffs are given "negotiating credits" for the decision even if the tariff is bound at a level above the currently applied level (as is the case for many developing economy participants in the Round). Bindings have also played a key role in establishing the domestic and international credibility of domestic reform programmes in many countries. Although an integral part of the tariff negotiations, bindings clearly are more akin to rules and procedures—in terms of their contribution to the predictability of future market access—than to direct increases in market access. However, even ceiling bindings yield significant benefits related to liberalisation when they reduce the expect value and variance of protection.

On the basis of data available for 26 developing countries, the GATT Secretariat has identified the main features of their market access commitments. These include: the expansion of bindings to cover 61 per cent of imports, compared to the pre-Uruguay Round level of 13 per cent. The increase in the security of trade among developing regions is reflected mainly in Latin America—where participants will bind 100 per cent of tariff lines at ceilings rates.

Too often, "market access" as used in descriptions of the Uruguay Round results is defined—implicitly or explicitly in a way that is too narrow and, even worse, mercantilist. The narrowness results from limiting the analysis of changes in market access to changes in tariffs and quotas. This overlooks three other key aspects of market access, namely the bindings of tariffs, the rules and disciplines on the use of other trade-related government interventions, and the institutional arrangements for monitoring and enforcing compliance with those disciplines. It is progress in these latter three areas that determines the security of increases in market access from reductions in tariffs and the elimination of quantitative restrictions. Since the gains from trade liberalisation depend heavily on the stimulus it provides to trade related investment, the security aspect is crucial.

Agricultural Products: Increased market access for agricultural products includes the "tariffication" of all non-tariff border measures (conversion to tariff-equivalents)—with the exception of those products for which special treatment has been negotiated—and a binding of all tariffs on agricultural products. As a result, the security of trade in agricultural products will for the first time be greater than in industrial products, since 100 per cent of agricultural product tarifflines will be bound.

Tariffs resulting from the "tariffication" process, together with the other tariffs on agricultural products, are to be reduced by a simple average of 36 per cent over six years in the case of developed countries and 24 per cent over ten years in the case of developing countries, with minimum reductions per tariff line of 15 per cent and 10 per cent, respectively. The reductions in the tariffs of developed countries—which account for about two-thirds of world imports of agricultural products—indicate an average percentage reduction of 37 per cent. With respect to individual product categories, developed countries will cut tariffs by above-average amounts on oilseeds, flowers an plants; and cut tariffs by below-average amounts on sugar and dairy products, with other product categories close to the average cut. In the categories of "topical products", which account for half of exports of developing countries of agricultural products, a 43 per cent reduction in tariffs will be implemented by developed countries.

Current access opportunities will be maintained on terms at least equivalent to those existing prior to the tariffication process. However, for those products where tariffication took place and imports were less than 5 per cent of domestic consumption because of the existing restrictions, minimum market access commitments, implemented through tariff quotas on an MFN basis at a low or minimal tariff rate, are required. Figures on the increased market access in terms of tonnage resulting from minimum access commitments indicate that substantial increases in market access occur for coarse grains (1,757,000) and rice (1,076,000 tons), as well as for other products. With regard to commitments on export competition, the quantities of exports which can be legally subsidized must be reduced by 21 per cent. Furthermore, total export subsidy outlays will decline by 36 per cent, from $21.3 billion to $13.7 billion by the end of the transition period. The importance of this commitment is that, on average, developed countries subsidized annually during 1986-90 48.2 million tons of wheat, 19.5 million tons of coarse grains, 1.8 million tons of sugar, 1.2 million tons of beef, etc. With regard to commitments on domestic support to agricultural producers, total outlays (in terms of the Aggregate Measurement of support) will be reduced by 18 per cent, from $197, billion to $162 billion by the end of the transition period.

The new market access opportunities for agricultural products which will result from the Uruguay Round—as a result of a change in border measures, and policies relating to export competition and domestic support—will be of particular interest to developing countries exporting temperature food products. More generally, multilateral disciplines on trade-distorting practices in agriculture are expected to stabilize world food markets in the coming decades, providing potential trade opportunities for developing countries and reducing fluctuations in food import bills, However, the potential situation in net food-importing developing countries is of particular concern. Potential problems relating to least-developed and net food importing developing countries are the subject of the Decision on *Measures Concerning the Possible Negative Effects of the Reform Programme on Least-Developed and Net Food Importing Developing Countries*. The Decision sets out objectives with regard to the provision of food aid, the provision of basic foodstuffs in full grant form and aid for agricultural development. It also refers to the possibility of assistance from the International Monetary Fund and the World Bank with respect to the short-term financing of food imports. The WTO Committee of Agriculture will monitor the implementation of the Decision.

WTO Agreements Covering Trade in Goods

GATT 1994: The cornerstone of trade relations in the area of goods. Differential and more favourable treatment to developing countries and to least-developed countries is permitted under the 1979 Enabling Clause with respect to tariffs in the context of the Generalized System of Preferences (GSP) and non-tariff measures, notwithstanding the most-favoured-nation clause, and with respect to regional or global arrangements concluded by developing countries.

Agreements Integrating Practices Otherwise on the Margin of GATT Rules: Includes trade-related investment measures (TRIMs) (which can be found to be inconsistent with the national treatment provision or the prohibition or quantitative restrictions), such as local content requirements or trade-balancing requirements. GATT inconsistent TRIMs are required to be notified and eliminated within a transition period of two years (developed countries), five years (developing countries) or seven years (least-developed countries). A further extension may be requested by developing ad least-developed countries. The Agreement on Safeguards prohibits the use of "grey-area measures", such as voluntary restraints or orderly marketing arrangements; such measures are to be notified and eliminated.

Agreement on Textiles and Clothing: Provides for the eventual elimination of the Multi-Fibre Arrangement (MFA) after a ten-year transition period. In place since 1973, the MFA currently groups eight "importers"; of these, Austria, Canada, the European Communities, Finland, Norway and the United States apply restrictions under the MFA, while Japan and Switzerland do not. The other participants in the MFA are the "exporters" (mainly developing countries), whose exports or part of their exports covered by the MFA are subject to bilaterally agreed quantitative restraints or unilaterally imposed restraints on imports, typically applied at the product level but in some cases to various aggregates as wells.

Trade in Services

The General Agreement on Trade in Services (GATS) is the first multilateral agreement on trade that has its objective the progressive liberalisation of trade in services. It provide for secure and more open market in services in a similar manner as the GATT has done for trade in goods. The Agreement covers trade in all service sectors and the supply of service in all forms.

The GATS has two components: the framework agreement containing 29 Articles and a number of Annexes, Ministerial Decisions etc., as well as the schedules of commitments undertaken by each Member to bind the existing degree of openness or remove existing restrictions.

Of importance to developing countries is the fact that virtually all Member have made commitments on the movement of natural persons, even if these are circumscribed by the requirement of intra-corporate transferee status. In addition, commitments made by developed countries generally cover the cross-border supply of labour-intensive services such as computer-related services, professional and construction services. Further, most developing countries have committed themselves to bind or liberalize tourism and travel service, including, for example, the liberalisation of foreign investment restrictions for hotel and resort operators. These commitments are likely to improve the supply capacity of this key sector, which provides the major source of foreign exchange earnings in a number of island developing countries and least-developed countries. In addition, a number of developing countries have taken the opportunity the GATS provides to schedule commitments, thereby binding their own domestic reform process. Improvements in the quality of service that will result from liberalisation and increased competition will contribute to improved efficiency, consumer welfare and growth in developing countries as well as all other countries.

Intellectual Property Rights

Under the WTO, the number of countries providing intellectual property protection will increase over time. Developed countries have one year to meet their obligations, developing countries have five years and least developed countries have eleven years, with the possibility of an extension. Special transitional arrangements apply in the situation where a developing country does not presently provide patent protection in a particular chemical.

Adherence to the Paris and Berne Conventions is fairly widespread among developing countries. Many developing countries already provide minimum standards of intellectual property protection on a national treatment basis, although the scope of such protection varies significantly. Potential benefits for developing countries emerging from the Uruguay Round include a framework more conducive to domestic research efforts and to technology transfer and foreign direct investment. There will, however, be additional administrative burdens of enforcing such rights (specifically dealt with under the TRIPS Agreement), potentially higher royalty payments and adjustment costs for industries which, in the absence of domestic legislation in the areas, were producing goods that would be considered as counterfeit in the future. These will also be requirements relating to patents which may well mean an increase in prices of certain goods in some developing countries. Pharmaceutical and agricultural products present examples. These increases are expected to be small, and there are provisions in the Agreement itself to minimize any adverse implications for developing countries.

Dispute Settlement

From the perspective of developing countries, it should be noted that the elements of the 1966 Decision on Dispute Settlement will continue to apply under the WTO dispute settlement procedures. Although this Decision has seldom been used, mainly because developing countries have only recently become more frequent users of the GATT dispute settlement procedures, it contains features of specific interest to developing countries, including automatic access to the "good offices" of the Director-General of the GATT/WTO to mediate and seek to find a satisfactory resolution to the dispute, and shorter time-limits in which panels must complete their deliberations.

Monitoring of Trade Policies

The TPRM provide for a Trade Policies Review Body to examine regularly the trade policies and practices of Members, every two years for the four major traders (the EU, US, Japan and Canada), every four years for the next sixteen leading traders, and every six years for the remaining traders, although longer intervals may be prescribed for least-developed countries.

The TPR process has helped countries assess their trade and economic reforms, and may have contributed to some portion of the liberalisation that has taken place under the Uruguay Round. In the future, the TPR process will help WTO Members evaluate their implementation of the Agreements, as well as provide an early warning of trends of potential concern to all participants in the trading system.

28

Rural Poverty in India

"It is morning in a remote farming area in India. As her husband harnesses a bullock to plough their field, a women pounds the grain she will use for the day's main meal. Three kilometres away, their children are collecting fuel wood and water before starting their morning walk to school".

"After School, they help their mother light a fire with a few sticks, milk the cow and collect the sundired grain. That evening, as the family rests around the hearth, father worries about how to sell his onions before they spoil and the price falls. Before sleeping his wife prepares a basket of home-grown vegetables to sell next day at the village market five kilometres away. With the takings, she hopes to buy a kerosene lamp although she might not have enough cash left to buy the kerosene immediately.."

That description of rural life is a daily reality for hundreds of millions of families throughout India. Rural poverty, 1990s means subsistence on the meagre earnings of wage labour or unreliable harvests from small plots of land. It means raising a family without safe drinking water or proper sanitation, suffering disease or injury without medical assistance. In times of unemployment or crop failure, it means living with the pangs of hunger—and the risk of death by famine.

Inside the Poverty Trap

Poverty in rural India is created and perpetuated by a number of closely interlined socio-economic processes.

1. Policies and institutional arrangements biased against the poor exclude them from the benefits of development, frustrate their productive potential and accentuate the impact of other poverty processes.

Institutional processes that perpetuate rural poverty include lack of access to land, inequitable share-cropping and tenancy arrangements, poor markets, limited access to credit, inputs and technology, and ineffective extension services. Other constraints are lack of training facilities, inadequate research related to smallholder farming system, and last but not least a lack of grassroots institutions needed to foster people's participation.

Policy and institutional biases have short and long-term impacts. In the short term, the poor are unable to earn enough to meet nutritional requirements or to take advantage of the market. "In the longer term", "poor households continue to lag behind because they do not generate a surplus for investment, nor do they have access to investment opportunities. Moreover, the rural poor may be forced to overuse resources, which undermines productivity and income".

2. Even today dualistic agrarian structures originating in colonial times persist. In Indian, highly capitalized large and medium-sized farms have virtually monopolistic control over land and labour at the expense of the small farm sector. Large scale commercial producers—control the best farm land. Resources have been funnelled into irrigated plantations producing cotton and mechanized cultivation of sorghum. In marginal areas, mechanisation has led to environmental degradation and the loss of seasonal grazing and stock routes for pastoralists.

"Thus, side by side with modern agriculture, millions of marginal farmers and herdsmen far below the poverty line". This dualism severely limits their capacity to grow food and accumulate capital. They lack marketable surpluses, and incentives and opportunities to save and invest.

3. Rapid population growth can cause and perpetuate rural poverty by increasing pressure on limited productive resources, social services and employment, as well as paradoxically—creating labour shortage through outmigration.

The most obvious consequence of rapid population growth is that, even with relatively high rates of economic growth, improvements in living conditions are limited. Total saving in the economy declines, leaving fewer resources for investment in human development. Negative consequence are most acute in rural areas. Growing population often combined with traditional laws of inheritance—has led to fragmentation of holdings, degradation of crop and pasture land, and falling yields. In areas with unequal distribution of land, rapid population growth has accelerated proletarisation of the rural work force and reduced incomes.

4. Rural poverty malnutrition and undernutrition are closely linked to environmental degradation. Poor people in marginal areas are destroying natural resources as they struggle to keep their production systems sustainable. In acute shortage of arable land has forced farmers to reduce the length of fallow periods and plough up land previously reserved for grazing. These practices have led to declining yields, soil depletion and further impoverishment. Population pressure is pushing weaker members of the rural community into ecologically vulnerable areas.

Degradation of the environment is strongly linked to household food insecurity and lack of fuel. Much of the fragile forest cover has been destroyed by poor rural people in the search for grazing land and fuel wood.

Government policies have also wrought environmental damage. A rapid expansion of areas under crops often accelerates deforestation and land degradation. Programmes to expand cereal production into marginal areas, subsidized capital to support commercial operations subsidies for inappropriate technologies and excessive transfer of income out of the agricultural sector may undermine the sustainability of smallholers and pastoralists' production systems.

Inadequate public investment in off-farm employment and infrastructure, a lack of price incentives and inadequate access to modern agricultural inputs and services discourage investment in land conservation, leading to further overuse and degradation.

5. As poverty undermines traditional social bond, the marginalisation of women has become a fact of rural life in India. With little or no access to land, million of women depend on casual employment on meagre wages. Often, they farm fragmented plots of poor quality. Limited access to inputs, extension, training and credit limits, in turn, their ability to enter commercial agriculture.

The exodus of males in search of work in urban areas (itself an indicator of poverty) has serious consequences for the women they have leave behind. Output from land often falls and less attention is paid to maintenance, setting the stage for a long-term decline in productivity. Many female headed households have abandoned the use of oxen for ploughing, some plough and plan late and other no longer weed their fields.

6. The ethnic or cultural marginalisation of tribal or minority populations also plays a role in poverty. Many of these groups are further threatened by newly marginalized groups as the expansion of cultivation reduces and grazing areas of nomadic herders.

7. Exploitative middles also perpetuate rural poverty Landlords exploit share croppers and tenants, moneylenders exploit debtors, and traders exploit small scale producers. During seasonal food shortages, the poor may have to borrow money at interests rates exceeding 20 per cent a month. Force to devote most of their energies to debt servicing, they sink deeper into the poverty trap.

In some cases, government controlled co-operatives and government agencies whose task is to protect the poor may themselves practise forms of exploitation. Heavy levies imposed by government agencies have damaged small farmers. Large, inefficient bureaucracies are paid for by the productive sectors of the community and frequently contribute to accumulation of large budget deficits.

8. Political troubles and civil strife have had a disastrous impact on the rural poor one effect is the disruption of development assistance to the rural poor, both from national and international agencies. Another is the transformation of many producers into consumers of social services with serious consequences for production, savings, capital accumulation and investment.

9. The international economic environment directly influences the well-being of the Indian poor. Falling commodity prices and projectionist policies in India affect the employment and incomes of plantation workers and smallholders producing for export, particularly those relying heaving on a few agricultural commodities. Change in international interest rates have repeatedly hurt smallscale producers in debt-burdened India, While world grain price increases has triggered rural famines.

The net flow of development resources to agriculture also affects rural poverty. Official development funding for food and agriculture increased between 1975 and 1982, but has fluctuated irregularly since. Moreover, concern with trade balance is diverting resources to export crops, sometimes at the expense of traditional crops grown by poor farmers.

29

Economics and Sustainable Development

Economics and ecologists were once seem as enemies: environmental protection, it was thought, could only be achieved at the expense of economic growth. The misconception persists at the extremes among both the most fundamentalist Greens and the most ideological free marketers. But increasingly it is now being recognized that development and care for the environment go hand in hand. This interdependence is coalescing in the new and necessary discipline of environmental economics.

Conventional economics patterns have often assumed that growth and technical progress will nullify all resource and environmental limits. Environmental economics recognizes that the world's natural capital underpins all development, and that it is rapidly becoming scarcer as human demands exceed the globe's long-term carrying capacity. Government of India has introduced environmental measures over the last two decades, but need to move further towards integrating them into economic policies. There can be no real sustainable development unless environment and development policies are integrated at the very beginning of the decision-making process.

Quantifying the Environmental Cost

One of the first steps is to work out the true costs of polluting and depleting the World's natural resources , such as its soil, air and water, the climate and the ozone layer. These have often been regarded as free goods, and it was believed that the world has an infinite capacity to absord the effects of human activities. Environmental economists, recognizing that the social and economic costs of degradating are very great, are trying to quantify them. They say that this will make possible better use of such tools as cost-benefit analysis, environmental impact assessment and risk assessment—and the production of national income accounts which reflect the depletion and degradation of natural resources. As these costs are identified and quantified, economic policy can increasingly be developed with sustainable development as the primary objective. Achieving sustainable development requires industrilized and developing countries to make dramatic changes in national and internatioal policies based on a global partnership. The greenhouse effect, the destruction of the ozone layer, the extinction of species and contamination of the oceans, and other environmental problems, affect us all, no matter which corner of the globe we inhabit.

The first and essential step in overcoming a difficulty is to recognize it and understand it. Concern over the difficulties related to sustainability has led scientists and national and international institutions to study the concept and suggest ways of meeting its many requirements. Indicators have been established to measure pollution levels, soil erosion, salinisation, deforestation and a host of environmental problems. Evaluating the impact of such natural resource—use on ecosystems is a major step towards finding the necessary solutions.

For example, it has become clear, on a macroeconomics level, that national accounting systems fail to reflect these effects adequately. Deterioration of the world's rivers, land degradation, air pollution and contamination of the seas are not taken into consideration. Inadequate accounting distorts reality and gives a falls idea of the true consequences of growth and production.

On a microeconomic level, much is being done to redefine production costs. Incorporating the cost of waste management and internalizing negative external impacts within production prices are beneficial aspects of the economics of sustainability.

Steps are being taken to evaluate public and commonly held assets and to put a price on them, even though they may not be subject to market forces. These are only in the earliest stage but they will allow for more accurate evaluation of the world's natural capital. Fiscal, market, quota and other instruments are being developed to enforce change in the way in which certain resources are used. Examples include markets for transferable emission quotas or compensatory taxation mechanisms designed to ensure that economic forces act to reduce greenhouse gas emissions. Efforts at impact analysis—and in a general sense, cost-benefit analysis—permit rough estimations of the impact that projects might have on ecosystems.

Long-term Repercussions

These instruments carry significant limitations but they are important nevertheless because they attempt to quantify impacts on the natural world and to achieve a more rational use of natural resources. The development of such instruments and evaluation techniques will have significant repercussions in the formulation of sustainable long-term policies. But we must bear in mind that sustainability is not just an economic issue: it is also a political and cultural one.

The concept of sustainability demands as alternative view point in which humankind and the natural world are perceived as a unit—as different yet mutually sustaining aspects of a whole. This perception is not incompatible with progress. It does not renounce development. It simply seeks to affirm life and refuses to discriminate between the means and the end. It understands that happiness cannot be achieved by destructive means. The questions of how to produce and how to consume therefor become extremely important. Neither should be at the expense of the future or of the natural world. Efficiency is not limited to the links between investment, products and prices: it must address the rational use of resources, including environmental and cultural consequences, both in the long and the short-term.

Very considerable adjustments must be made in the interests of sustainable development. They demand a reassessment of all our activities which cannot, logically, be done overnight. It is a long and continuous process, characterized by steadfastness and compromise.

30

Solving the Unemployment Problem by Looking Beyond the Job

If you had a job, you worked; if you didn't, you didn't. Having a job meant being employed by an organisation in a clearly—defined and stable occupational role, with duties, hours, rates of pay and promotion all more or less standardized. But the job—in that meaning of the world—is a social invention, and a fairly recent one.

The job—the kind that you had, or hoped to get—became a central fixture of life. Its importance was great because it served many needs: For managers and efficiency experts, job assignments were the key to assembly-line manufacturing. For union organizers, jobs protected the rights of workers. For political reformers, standardized civil service positions were the essence of good government. Jobs provided an identify to immigrants and recently, urbanized farm workers. They provided a sense of security for individuals and an organizing principle for society.

Jobs functioned in so many ways that it is surprising how many organisations are now opting for other ways to define and manage work. The second job shift is underway. Its emergence can be seen in the increasing use of temporary and part-time workers and contracted-out services, the changing relationships between workers and management, the growing popularity of self-employment and small business. Indeed, "de-jobbing" is proceeding at such a pace that many economists, management experts and futurists are now talking freely about the end of the job. Bridges predicts that the job as we now know it will disappear entirely—replaced by new kinds of flexible work assignments in post-job organisations—and be remembered only as a quaint artifact of the industrial age.

One reason for the change in work is the economic rules of the survival game among organisations that employ workers. To stay successful in today's hitech consumer economy, businesses have had to re-model themselves into what some experts call "agile companies"—ones that are able to respond quickly to conditions in ever-changing fragmenting, competitive markets.

The "knowledge worker", whose work involves not simply doing something, but also applying theoretical or analytical skills. Such workers are replacing the industrial labourer as the dominant part of the workforce—and their productive activities are likely to be organized and structured much differently from those of their assembly-line predecessors.

De-jobbing as a result of new technology or the emergence of a service economy is a phenomenon that gets a lot of attention these days; but it is not the whole story. At all levels of society, people are improvising livelihoods that do not fit the industrial-era model. Immigrants to the developed countries, often unable to find steady jobs, nevertheless find places in the new landscape by being mobile, flexible, resourceful and imaginative; they moonlight, work, part-time, share jobs, start small businesses. Their lives are often extremely difficult, but they are also instructive to those of us believe you either have a job or you're out of luck.

It is too early to evaluate the implications of this multifaceted transformation of work, or to dismiss it as simply good or bad. Nevertheless, one cannot deny that it is taking place, and will bring about dramatic social changes.

On the downside, the job shift is causing great hardships for many workers and their families. It poses serious challenges to policy-makers, political activists and labour leaders. The basic question appears to be whether the key to global employment-development strategy is to play "catch-up"—trying to bring millions of people around the world into jobs in industries and the public sectors; or to play "leapfrog"-creating new forms of employment.

The proposal to generate more employment in agriculture, for example, is based on new demand for agricultural exports from developing countries. The policies designed to make the most of this opportunity include measures to upgrade technology, raise productivity, ensure the supply of essential inputs, establish marketing and distribution channels, create links between agriculture and industry, and cater to export markets.

The issue of part-time work, another kind of employment that is seriously undervalued in the traditional industrial—era job mind-set. Part-time work may not offer much at this point to developing countries, where many people are under employed and wages are low, but it can be of great help in more advanced economies. And it is likely to be a big part of the global work picture in the years ahead.

A certain agility may also be necessary in agriculture, particularly in countries that for many years have depended heavily on producing commodities such as sugar for export as a means of generating income and employment. As Northern laborations develop non-agricultural substitutes for many of these commodities—and this is already beginning to happen—the bottom may fall out of "monoculture" economies, only economic, but will have long-run political implications as communities attempt to reorganize themselves in response to the changed conditions. It is, therefore, in the interest of raw materials exporters to closely monitor current trends in biotechnology and the use of genetic resources and modify their internal policies in anticipation of potential long-term effects."

This calls for flexibility, and an ability to get information and to act on it. Government officials, development workers, community leaders and individuals will, in some respects, all have to be "knowledge workers" if they are to keep ahead of global changes. Jobs are going to be created not just by putting people to work, but by finding-or creating-new niches where they can be productive.

It is still possible to talk about jobs for all, and to resist the assumption made by many economists that high levels of unemployment are now inevitable. But, as we move ahead into the global information economy, we may be moving back into an older conception of the job, and seeing it again as something you do, rather than as something you have—or that has you.

31

Social Summit

The issues which the World Summit for Social Development is called upon to tackle—poverty, unemployment and social exclusion—are among the most critical of our time. In spite of the considerable material gains that have been registered during the past 50 years, in spite of the tremendous technological progress that has been achieved, in spite of the more favourable international political climate resulting from the end of the Cold War, poverty continues to grow and inequalities continue to widen.

Over a billion people are living in poverty. Some 30 per cent of the world's labour force is not productively employed. Many societies are being torn apart by racial, ethnic and religious conflict and intolerance. These social issues constitute the greatest threat to peace, stability and prosperity in today's world and need to be tackled with urgency and determination by policy-makers at the highest level.

If the Social Summit is to leave its mark on history, it will have to be more than a ritual gathering of Heads of State and Government. It will have to result in a perceptible improvement in the social situation in countries throughout the world—in the short and medium term, not in some indefinite future.

It will have to acknowledge that these are truly global problems which require global action in a world characterized by growing inter-dependence. National action, important though it is, will no longer suffice.

A collective commitment by all the nations of the world to the goal of full, productive and freely chosen employment is of crucial importance to the work of the Summit. It is only through their labour that individuals can contribute to the creation of wealth for their benefit and for society as a whole, can lift themselves out of poverty, can be integrated into social, economic, political and cultural life.

In view of the growing globalisation of the economy—characterized by freer trade and capital movements and greater exposure to world market forces—no country acting alone can achieve full employment without a favourable international economic environment. But we also expect emphasis to be laid on appropriate national strategies: macro-economic policies, industrial and agricultural policies which favour the growth of job-creating enterprises, education and training policies, active labour market policies which enable individuals and enterprises to adjust rapidly to changing market conditions, and policies which grant all citizens equal access to employment, education and training.

We expect the Summit to commit all nations to take special action to improve the employment prospects of those who are in a particularly disadvantaged position in the labour market—young people, disabled people, ethnic minorities. We expect it to recognize the special contribution made by women to the general welfare—through their role in the family and in production—and to end the pervasive discrimination and inequality still suffered by women.

We expect the Summit to emphasize that full employment does not mean the creation of any sort of jobs, but of high-quality jobs. We expect it to recognize the basic rights of workers—freedom of association and collective bargaining, freedom from forced labour, equal pay for work of equal value, equality of opportunity in employment and occupation.

We expect it to recognize the importance of measures which provide social security and minimum wages, which protect against arbitrary dismissal and which ensure occupational safety and health.

However balance has to be struck between the need for adequate protection and incomes on the one hand and need not to price workers and enterprises out of the market on the other. Realistic and socially acceptable solutions can only be found if those most directly concerned—employers and workers—are fully involved in decision-making on these matters through organisations of their own choosing.

Finally, and perhaps most important of all, we expect the Summit to determine the institutional framework and mechanisms for following up its conclusions. There is no point in adopting fine-sounding commitments and policies if there is no means of ensuring and monitoring follow-up action.

If the Summit fails to establish such a framework, its conclusions could well prove to be a hollow text that will quickly be forgotten.

32

Tapping the Market: *Can Private Enterprise Supply Water to the Poor?*

Over 170 million people have no access to clean water in urban areas throughout the world. Inefficient operation of state owned water companies is at the root of this injustice: gross over-staffing and political interference in tariff-setting have starved utilities of the resources needed to expand piped networks to impoverished areas.

The failure of the supply-driven approach has led to public private partnership (PPPs) designed to shift water utilities towards a demand-driven approach. Have these changes been accompanied by improved access to clean, affordable water for the urban poor? Has PPP improved equity in urban water supply? Are the new private sector operators addressing the needs of the urban poor in practice? This article examines the extent to which the urban poor have benefited or not from this newly emerging institutional arrangement.

The 'public' approach typically provides unclean water sporadically. It requires expensive, highly educated professionals, significant subsidies and tends to service clients on high and middle incomes whilst changing low tariffs. International financial institutions have failed to enable the public water suppliers to improve performance, either through massive investment in engineering, or through capacity building and institutional development.

At the other extreme is an efficient, demand driven, customer-oriented approach, the 'small scale independent providers', delivering water to cities' inhabitants, with near 100 per cent bill collection efficiency. Promoting local employment and servicing the poor, this approach has, until recently, been ignored by water sector professionals. Lacking regulatory oversight, however, their prices are typically 10 to 20 times higher than those paid by high-income consumers connected to the network. Which of these providers are most effective at serving the poor? The starting point is to recognise the evidence suggesting that the urban poor are prepared to pay to meet their survival and convenience needs for water.

Notwithstanding the rhetoric to the contrary by some trade unions and NGOs, initial results from larger cities indicate that the efficiency of 'privatised' water utilities has improved markedly: leakages are down and net revenue is up through improved billing and collection and reduction in personnel. Whether this is due to the alleged benefits of private sector investment or the freedom of foreign operators to manage without being beholden to employee and entrenched political interests is not yet clear.

Has the Extension of the Network to Poor Communities Been Speeded Up?

Concession contracts require private operators to meet coverage targets. But the decision on the direction of network expansion to meet targets are usually left to the operators as regulatory bodies are usually formed after contract signing. So are poor communities given priority? Technical criteria based on cost-effectiveness in the construction of main pipes, commercial criteria based on pressure from property developers, and political criteria based on vote-winning tactics may all conflict with social criteria based on the pressing needs of poor communities.

Is the Cost of Household Connection Affordable by the Poor?

Even where operators do give priority to extending the piped network into poor communities, difficult issues arise over the financing of secondary pipelines, household connections and meter installation. Techniques are evolving to reduce the cost of connection so as to ensure affordability for all. These may take the form of tripartite arrangements whereby the public sector provides grants for the purchase of materials, community groups provide voluntary labour, and the private operator provides technical assistance. NGOs may contribute by providing crucial skills in team management and local understanding not usually found in the bureaucratic culture of public sector institutions or the techno-professional culture of private water companies.

Is the Water Tariff Affordable by the Poor?

Even where poor communities have been connected, there is no assurance that householders can afford the water charges. Many have no job security or regular income. Billing arrangements need to be shortened from the monthly norm to fit the short-term financial horizon imposed by household poverty.

Property-based tariff structures still discriminate against the poor by providing far cheaper water per litre for high-income households consuming large volumes for swimming pools and sprinkler systems. Reforms should positively discriminate in favour of the poor, with some cross-subsidisation from richer to poorer households. However, where the initial life-line block is greater than average monthly domestic water use by the poor (perhaps over $6m^3$ per household a month), middle income groups benefits the most. A single volumetric tariff for domestic consumers with subsidies aimed at facilitating water connections rather than consumption is now being recommended.

This article focuses on the three major challenges for the sector in the new millennium.

- First it is crucial to develop regulatory skills to oversee this affordable expansion. The key capacity constraints facing municipalities—usually the public sector partners in PPPs.
- Second is the need to incorporate the skills of small-scale independent providers.

- Thirdly it is important to move beyond the metropolitan capitals, to where cross-subsidies are more achievable, and address the water needs of the urban poor in the myriad of secondary towns in the south.

33

The Trade Related Intellectual Property Rights (TRIPS) Agreement and the Developing Countries

The basic norms of free competition established in the nineteenth century induced legislators to provide relatively week forms of intellectual property protection. Often innovators could rely only on such factors as lead time, reputation for quality and continuing technical improvements to maintain their foothold in the market.

Undermining this outlook were two developments that led to the inclusion of intellectual property issues in the World Trade Organisation (WTO). First, the rise of knowledge-based industries radically altered the nature of competition and disrupted the equilibrium that had resulted from more traditional comparative advantages. Second, the growing capacity of manufacturers in developing countries to penetrate distant markets for traditional industrial products forced the developed countries to rely more heavily on their comparative advantages in the production of intellectual goods than in the past. Market access for developing countries thus became a bargaining chip to be exchanged for greater protection of intellectual goods within a restructured global market place.

Since 1986 the developed countries' drive for extraterritorial protection of intellectual property rights has largely ignored the competitive capabilities of developing countries with respect to intellectual goods, and it has also downplayed these countries' rights to preferential treatment under existing rules. At the same time, the logic of multilateral trade negotiations skews the pre-existing North-South conflict over intellectual property rights by introducing the prospects of trade concessions in unrelated fields. Intellectual property rights constitute but one of many variables that bear on competitive capacity and the transfer of technology in general.

Primary Intellectual Property Regimes

Patents

The extension of patentability to virtually all types of technology recognized by developed patent systems, the prolongation of patent protection to a uniform term of twenty years, and legal recognition of the patentee' exclusive rights to import the relevant products could adversely affect developing countries whose existing patent laws fall below these standards. In practice, however, the competitive status of any given developing country in a post-TRIPS world will depend in part on the level of foreign direct investment it attracts and on the benefits that strengthened intellectual property rights bring to domestic innovators.

Competition under stronger patent regimes requires developing countries to adopt legal means of narrowing the scope of foreign patent monopolies and of encouraging local entrepreneurs either to work around the claimed inventions or to develop improvements suited to local conditions. To this end, local entrepreneurs should exploit technical information in disclosures published abroad; patent authorities should exercise all of the claims limitations practised abroad; and domestic courts should strictly interpret the doctrine of equivalents. Legislative enactments of utility model laws would provide additional incentives to adapt foreign inventions to local conditions and to improve them further.

Moreover, unpatented traditional technologies will often remain suitable for local needs, and the resulting products may be sold at lower prices than imported products of patented technologies. Entrepreneurs in developing countries should also be prepared to exploit unpatented applications of applied scientific know-how in such advanced technologies as biogenetic engineering and computer programme-related innovation.

In time, increased direct investment by foreign patentees could enable developing-country licensees who exploit their natural advantages, especially low labour costs, to succeed on both domestic and export markets where non-licensees were unable or unwilling to venture in the past. Familiarisation with the benefits of the patent system should stimulate greater investment in domestic research and development and in technological innovation.

The gradual extension of patents to new technologies such as computer programmes ad bio-genetic engineering without the emergence of agreed international minimum standards creates both opportunities and risks for the developing countries. While the developed countries enjoy unique advantages in biotechnology that only become available to developing countries as a consequence of stronger patent systems, some developing countries may find their own competitive status enhanced by the provision of proprietary rights, including plant breeders' rights, though others may not. The patenting of biogenetic advances decreases the scope for reverse-engineering and could also increase the costs of doing business in key sectors of some developing economies, notably agriculture. As regards information technologies, reliance on copyright and trade secrets at the international level appears less unfavourable to the developing countries' prospects than patents, for reasons that are set out below. However, the tendency to patent software could diminish these prospects by posing limits to reverse engineering and to the attainment of the interoperability, and this trend adds to the overall costs of disseminating information goods.

To the extent that patented technology is not made available on reasonable terms of that un-wholesome economic dependencies actually arise, developing countries will have to consider measures to restore the competitive balance that are consistent with the TRIPS Agreement. For example, the agreement allows compulsory licences when the rights holders fail to licences patented technology "on reasonable commercial terms". It also provides other bases for defensive regulatory action by emphasizing "the transfer and dissemination of technology, to the mutual advantage of producers and users" and the need "to promote the public interest in sectors of vital importance to socio-economic and technological development".

Measures to restrain abuses of intellectual property rights as authorized by the Paris Convention also remain available under the TRIPS agreement, which expressly empowers developing countries to deal with licencing practices that "adversely affect the international transfer of technology".

Finally, the agreement specifically preserves the right of all states to "adopt measure necessary to protect public health and nutrition and to promote the public interest in sectors of vital importance to socio-economic and technological development, provided that such measures are consistent with the provisions of this agreement".

Trademarks and Geographical Indications

The TRIPS provisions give pre-existing norms greater specificity while softening the use requirement and eliminating both compulsory licences and local linkage requirements. These provisions also subject the international regime of trade-marks and unfair competition to more stringent enforcement measures, including border controls against imports of counterfeit goods.

As a result, developing countries will need to reassess the pro-competitive functions of trade marks in open economies while addressing questions of abuse in a more direct fashion. They should insist on receiving the technical cooperation and aid that the TRIPS agreement envisages for the purpose of defraying administrative and enforcement burdens.

Governments should consider policies and incentives that encourage enterprises to establish their own market identities through appropriate trademarks and foreign firms to allow licensees to adopt more of the licenced products for both domestic and export needs under local trademarks.

Copyrights

Authors in many developing countries are very active in both domestic and foreign markets. It nonetheless remains true that the balance of trade in cultural goods favours exports from developed countries. This imbalance could increase under the TRIPS agreement, which generally applies the international minimum standards of the Berne convention, plus selected standards from the Rome convention on neighbouring rights.

While efforts to implement these standards is mandatory, developing country authorities should familiarize themselves with the extent to which the scope of copyright protection varies from country to country, in the absence of authoritative legal limitations recognized by international law. Carefully framed public-interest exceptions may further reduce the overall costs of a TRIPS Agreement without violating international copyright norms. Moreover, the revised Berne Convention already provides for compulsory licences for educational and scientific test, and developing countries may wish to consider making greater use of these concessions.

Ancillary Proprietary Regimes

Trade Secrets

In modern economies trade secret law regulates the pace of competition by endowing second comers with an absolute right to reverse-engineer. To operate successfully under such a regime, developing countries must realign the concept of "transfer of technology" with the nature of competition on open markets. Technology is transferred through self-help methods of reverse engineering. The potential benefits of reverse-engineering unpatented technologies increase when advanced technologies are involved, notably biogenetic engineering, computer programmes and computer-aided design. The unpatented, non-copyrightable know-how underlying these technologies is often embodied in tangible products available to the pubic, which renders classical trade secret protection of doubtful efficacy. By ignoring this problem, the TRIPS Agreement provides entrepreneurs in developing countries with major opportunities, notwithstanding the extension of trade secret law under TRIPS, provided they are willing and able to master the art of reverse-engineering.

Other Proprietary Regimes

The TRIPS Agreement mandates intellectual property protection for industrial designs, plant varieties and integrated circuit designs. Although the developed countries enjoy a clear advantage in advanced sectors of industrial design, more traditional sectors rooted in aesthetic appeal rather than technical efficiency remain accessible to firms in developing countries.

Need for Multilateral Policies

Global economic integration increasingly requires that intangible creations receive minimum international standards of legal protection. Purely territorial intellectual property rights will thus give way to international sovereignty. However, then norms, of that law represent a delicate balance between the interests of States at different stages of development, so that the evolution of international intellectual property law will have to accommodate these norms and that balance.

Efforts to implement higher intellectual property standards will put increasing strains on competition law, which is not directly covered by the TRIPS Agreement. Identifying the parameters of healthy competition valid for all players in an integrated world market will become a pressing task for the international community in a post-TRIPS world. These issues will be complicated by the fact that innovators, users, and second comers all have different stakes in fashioning the rules of unfair competition law, and their interests will increasingly vary more with their economic roles than with the geopolitical affiliations of their respective national States.

Competition law must, become an integral part of international discussions of intellectual property rights, and there is a great need for multilateral cooperation to achieve a marketwide balance between incentives to create, and reasonable opportunities to imitate and improve upon, technological innovation. These discussions should lead to an internationally agreed framework for promoting a transfer of technology that is compatible with the drive for greater economic efficiency. To the extent that such cooperation succeeds, it will contribute a new perspective to the notion of fair competition that should strengthen the prospects of all participants in the global marketplace.

34

What's Driving Migration

The scale and diversity of today's migrations are beyond any previous experience. Rapid urban growth and environmental degradation in rural areas have led to internal migration affecting hundreds of millions of people. Migration is now seen as a priority issue equal in political weight to other major global challenges such as the environment, population growth and economic imbalances between regions.

Families and households from the basis for economic growth, social development and personal fulfilment. Decisions, by individual women and men on marriage, family, a place to live, shape the destinies of communities and nations. National policies and international conditions provide the context for individual decision-making. Effective development policies, including population, reproductive health and family planning policies, address this reality.

Data on national an global population trends set the agenda for national policy. An important element of population programmes is gathering data that will allow policy-making responsive to the realities of daily life, and to the needs and aspirations of individuals.

The dominant feature of global demographics is still growth. Age distribution is a growing concern, as the numbers of young and elderly people, grow, relative to the working-age population. The world is growing steadily more urban. From being a sign of strength and dynamism in the national economy, the rate and scale of urban growth has become increasingly a cause for concern. The influx of migrants to the biggest cities may be weakening both urban and rural sectors.

International migration is small in extent compared with internal movements, but has a disproportionate impact. Both internal and international migration are driven by population growth, and by inequities between countries. Migration is one of the choices which shape people's lives and the destiny of nations. But it can also be a symptom of inequity and underdevelopment. Migrants are by definition the most vulnerable members of the host community. The living and working conditions should be protected.

Open and frank exchange of information and views between host and sending countries is needed more than ever. The aim of the international community should be to protect the right to move, but to ensure that movement is voluntary and that it stimulates rather than holds back personal an national development. "The point of departure should be the human right to live and work where one pleases so long as it does not infringe on other people's right to do the same."

The Urban Transformation

The rural sector is declining in importance and its contribution to national economies. It is increasingly part of a unified economy based on the city. Contact with the urban areas is easier than ever and is encouraged by rural development.

Temporary and circular migration is giving way to more permanent settlement. The largest cities are under increasing strain, and residents are encountering increasing difficulties in improving or even maintaining living conditions. Nevertheless migration continues driven by a variety of forces both positive and negative. The choice to move can be part of a strategy for survival or personal development; but it is often enforced by external conditions.

The urban transformation is irreversible, but rural sectors must also be strengthened to balance the developing economy. Attention to gender issues will be crucial in ensuring a successful transition. The forces driving internal and international migration have much in common. Demographic pressures are contributing to both. As the pressures encouraging migration increase, the options for migrants become more limited. This collision is contributing to the atmosphere of crisis surrounding both urban and international migration.

Costs and Benefits

Migration is the result of individual or family decisions. But it is also part of social process. In economic terms migration is as much a global phenomenon as trade in commodities or manufactured goods. It is part of a broader pattern, and evidence of changing economic, social and cultural relationships.

But migration may be evidence of a different kind of relationship: the combination of poverty, rapid population growth and environmental damage is a powerful destabilizing factor driving urban growth and eventually international migration. On the recipient side, migration has usually been seen as evidence of a thriving economy: today's industrial states were built in part by migrant labour, skills and investment. In today's increasingly uncertain conditions, migration may be seen as a threat to the security and well-being of the local workforce and society at large. The only effective means to reduce migration pressures over the long term are to slow population growth; to stimulate economic growth and job creation at home, and promote the development of the individual and the family as the basic economic and social unit.

A Question of Gender

It is often assumed that most migrants are men, in reality, women make up nearly half of the international migrant population. Gender differences in social and economic roles affect migration decision making, household strategy, and the sex composition of labour migration. Attention to the gender dimension of migratory movements ought to be an important component in population and development planning.

Women frequently take the initiative in migration decisions, which may reflect limited opportunities in rural areas. Low status limits women's choices at home and may increase pressure to migrate, but it may also affect life in the host community. Opportunities may be limited by lack of education or skills, or by customer limitation on women's freedom of action outside the family or ethnic group. Paid employment for migrant women is usually in the lowest wage, least secure, and lowest status jobs, mostly in housework, child care and trade.

Most educated women end up in the same low-status, low-wage production and service jobs as unskilled female migrants. Men, too, experience downward mobility, but the contrast in the decline in women's employment status is far greater. Despite these disadvantages women migrants have become significant economic actors. Their status may be improved by migration, but the advantages are not clear-cut. Women's status as migrants is affected by their vulnerability, and by their lack of reproductive freedom. To ensure improved status they will need both legal protection and essential services, including reproductive health services.

Refugees

Refugees in the 1990s are overwhelmingly in Asia, Africa and Latin America. Their numbers are large, about 17 million, and growing rapidly. A further 3.5 to 4 million were thought to be in "refugee-like situations", though estimates are probably extremely conservative, and an estimated 23 million people internally displaced.

It is important to recognize the common roots of refugee and other forms of mass movement of populations. At the same time, despite the difficulty of distinguishing between political and socio-economic causes of migration, there is a clear need to distinguish between refugees and other groups of migrants. Participation in international efforts of burden-sharing would ensure that most refugee problems would be dealt with in their regions of origin.

Conclusions and Policies

Migration highlights linkages and interdependencies within countries, with many implications for development agendas, including population programmes and development assistance.

Policies to regulate or moderate international migration have concentrated largely on urban growth. They have been only intermittently effective. The most successful have concentrated on stimulating rural development and the growth of alternative urban centres.

Migration is also a personal or family decision, which is affected by external conditions such as poverty or environmental degradation, improving conditions of personal and family decisions, it can be influenced by policies that improve the quality of life.

This offers the opportunity for policies emphasizing individual development, among them education, health (including reproductive health) and family planning. Such policies are particularly relevant to the Strategies must take into account gender differences in social and economic life and the differential effects of policies.

Migration decisions are about family security and long-term-life-chance, rather than simply the maximisation of income. They are ultimately strategies designed to look after the individual's and the house needs, safeguard their security, and respond to their aspirations. If the goal is to reduce migration pressures through development it will be essential to increase the capacity but reduce the need to migrate. Long-term external support will be required to make such policies a reality, particularly in areas of rapid population growth and potential mass outward flows. Highly coordinated allocation of development assistance can help establish priorities and focus attention on basic needs. The challenge to both international donors and co-operating government is to direct programme spending to the areas where it can be most effective.

35

Crisis Prevention: *Can Better Development Planning Lessen the Toll of Civil Emergencies and Natural Disasters?*

Even a cursory scan of the world's headlines is depressing: armed conflicts are grinding on in Somalia, Afghanistan and in a growing number of other countries. And the effects of natural disasters are becoming more catastrophic each year. International relief aid, in response to such emergencies, has increased substantially. But how large can these sums of money realistically be expected to grow? With no end in sight to the need for relief, the good will of international donors is quickly giving way to disillusionment.

This leads us to a second question, which is, where does development fit in this grim scenario? For the development community to remain aloof from the issue of disasters and emergencies is not only politically short-sighted, it also ignores totally the causes and the effects of such phenomena.

Natural hazards such as hurricanes and earthquakes may be impossible to prevent. But they only become natural disasters if people are vulnerable. Why is it, for example, that an earthquake in Khilari, Maharashtra that registered 6.9 on the Richter scale killed up to 35,000 people, when an earthquake of almost the exact same magnitude in Los Angeles in 1994 claimed only 57 lives? By reducing poverty we can help increase the coping capacity of vulnerable populations. Therefore helping people lower such vulnerability is as much a development issue as the environment, or women's participation in development. Moreover, the repercussions of natural disasters go far beyond the immediate casualty list that so transfixes the media. Secondary and longer-term effects cab be equally if not more devastating. And they must be taken into account by development practitioners.

It has been estimated, for example, that the damage to Mexico City's infrastructure form a massive 1985 earthquake amounted to US$ 3.6 billion. Yet over the subsequent five years, the negative ripple effect on that country's balance of payments resulted in a loss of $8.6 billion. Furthermore, reconstruction requirements forced Mexcian authorities to revise their economic policies to meet an increased demand for public funding, credits and imports. The priorities for public expenditure were redirected to reconstruction projects, leaving many of the pre-disaster problems of the city and its people unattended.

In Bangladesh, floods in the recent past 2,000 people. But on closer examination we find that the toll was much more extensive than that: in each o these years the country's economic growth rate was halved by the delayed planting of rice and the destruction of seedbeds in the floods, further undermining the country's food security. All of these are consideration that go beyond relief, but they must be taken into account by development professionals.

Other emergencies may be more complex, but must be subjected to the same analysis. As the situations in Angola, Burundi, Somalia and the former Yugoslavia demonstrate, we know little about the dynamics of emergencies that arise from civil conflict. We do know, however that their cause usually lies in a lethal mix of poverty, poor governance and ethnic or religious rivalries exacerbated by profound social inequities. We are also learning that their resolution frequently requires the application of peacekeeping and political measures, combined with relief and development. Among the most virulent effects of such complex emergencies is the massive displacement of people; women and children are the principal victims, constituting 70 per cent of the world's refugees.

These complex emergencies around the world could easily get worse before they get better. This being said, carefully designed development efforts—carried out as building blocks to national reconciliation in the fragile post-conflict stage will need to increase commensurately. The appropriateness and the sustainability of these development efforts will be one of the most important factors in determining whether peace itself becomes sustainable. For example, the absence of carefully tailored reintegration strategies for demoblized soldiers and their host communities would be an almost open invitation to resumed violence.

Yet we must also be conscious of the impact of aid and try harder to prevent the need for relief in the first place. An increasing body of evidence suggests, for example that emergency aid can sometimes be counter-productive in the longer term, increasing the vulnerability of populations and impeding recovery. Ironically, we find ourselves in situation today where it is far easier to obtain funds for maintaining refugees in their place of asylum than for helping them reintegrate into their own societies. In such cases, we may very well be helping to perpetuate the problem that we sought to relieve, as the presence of large numbers of refugees is sometimes itself a cause of conflict.

So how are we to proceed? And what exactly is the nature of the relief to development continuum that remains logical in the abstract but elusive in reality? The concept of a continuum does not imply a linear and absolutely progressive set of responses. On the contrary, it means that we are dealing with a set of processes rather than rigidly defined steps. It also means that development must be very much part of the disaster management process, and that the aim of the continuum must be to move from relief to rehabilitation and resumed development at the earliest opportunity. However, this resumed development must include conscious measures to reduce the vlunerability that caused the disaster or the emergency in the first place.

In other words, we must give greater thought to prevention before we reach for the "cure"—for humanitarian, political an financial reasons. (The Japanese insurance alone). And as development paractitioners, we must reconcile ourselves to the vastly more complicated environment in which we have to operate.

This means, for example that we will have to begin examining whether the economic policy "medicine" often prescribed will reduce conflict or enhance it. We will have to ask ourselves if the reconstruction period following a civil conflict or natural disaster is the right time to advocate cuts in social spending, as has happened in certain countries in Africa and Latin America. Similarly, is it really in children's best interests to build a school in a seismic zone without first ensuring its structural stability? And does it really make sense to urge drought-prone countries to increase their reliance on cash crops, as has been done in some instances.

A story that never made headlines anywhere involves hundreds of the poorest people in Bangladesh, whose homes remained intact during the floods of 1988, when many others were simply washed away. these people were fortunate enough to have obtained credit through the Grameen Bank for construction materials as well as instruction in the building of flood-resistant homes. The Grameen revolving fund had received start-up capital from International Financial Agencies. Since that time the effort has been expanded, and more than 10,500 flood-resistant homes have been built in the last two years.

This is just one example of the kind of action we need more of in fairly predictable and recurring circumstances such as the floods in Bangladesh, as well as in the more complex, man-made emergencies to which we must respond.

Bibliography

Books

A. C. Pigou (1960). *The Economics of Welfare*, Macmillan & Co. Ltd., London.

Ahluwalia Montek, S. (1985). *Rural Poverty, Agricultural Production and Prices: A Re-Examination* in John Mellor and Desai Gunvant, M. (eds.) "Agricultural Changes and Rural Poverty", The John Hopkins University Press, London.

Amartya Sen (1995). *The Hindu*, 6th November, Interviewed by Ramamanohar Reddy, Chennai.

Betellei, A. (2000). *Chronicles of Over Time*, Penguine Books, New Delhi.

Carr, Maryn et al., (1997). Speaking Out; *Women's Economic Empowerment in South Asia,* Vikas Publications, New Delhi.

Chakravarthy Sukamoy (1989). *Development Planning, The Indian Experience*, Oxford University Press, New Delhi.

Charsely, S. R. and G. K. Karanth (1998). *Challenging Untouchability, Dalit Initiative and Experience from Karnataka*, Sage Publications, New Delhi.

Chinnadurai, K. (1986). *Evaluation Study of Implementation* of IRDO, State Bank of India, Coimbatore.

Dantwala, M. L. (1996). *Dilemmas of Growth*: the Indian Experience, Sagar Publications; New Delhi.

Delige R. (1999). *The Untouchables of India*, Berg, New York.

Desai, B. M. and N. V. Namboodiri (1993). *Rural Financial Institutions: Promotion and Performance*, Oxford and IBH Publishing Company Pvt. Ltd., New Delhi.

Dev, S. Mahendra (1999). *State Interventions and Women's Employment*, in T. S. Papola and Alakh N. Sharma (Eds) (1999). "Gender and Employment in India"; Vikas Publishing House Pvt. Ltd., New Delhi, pp. 373-411.

Dharm Narain & Sen, A. K. et al. (1989). *Studies on Indian Agriculture*, Oxford University Press, New Delhi.

Frencine Fournier (1997). *Foreword, Poverty and Participation in Civil Society*. Edited by Yogesh Atal of Else Oyen, Abhinav Publications, New Delhi.

George Psacharopoulos and Moureen Woodhall (1986). *Education for Development; An, Analysis of Investment Choices,* Oxford, New York.

Griffin (1979). *The Political Economy of Agrarian Change,* The MacMillan Press Ltd., London.

Griffin Keith (1978). *International Inequality and National Poverty,* The Macmillan Press Ltd., London.

Griffin Keith (1981). *Land Concntration and Rural Poverty,* The Macmillan Press Ltd:, Hong Kong.

Gunnar Myrdal (1968). *Asian Drama—An Inquiry into Poverty of Nations,* Pantheon, New York.

Gunnar Myrdal (1970). *The Challenge of World Poverty, A World Anti-Poverty Programme in Outline,* Pantheon, New York.

Gupta, D. (2000). *Interrogating Caste: Understanding Heirarchy and Difference in Indian Society,* Penguine Books, New Delhi.

Haq, Mahabub Ul. (1978). *The Poverty Curtain: Choices for the Third World,* Oxford University Press, Bombay.

Haq, Mahabub Ul. (1997). *Human Development in South Asia,* Oxford University Press, New York.

Harper, M. (1998). *"Profit for the Poor"*, Oxford and IBH Publishing Co., Delhi.

Hirway Indira (1984). *Programmes for Poverty Eradication: A Critique of Target Group Approach,* Sardar Patel Institute for Economic and Social Research (Mimeo).

Holcombe, Susan(1995). *Managing to Empower; The Grameena Bank's Experience of Poverty Alleviation*, Oxford University Press Dhaka.

IFMR (1984). *An Economic Assessment of Poverty Eradication and Rural Unemployment Alleviation Programme and their Prospects,* Madras.

Jackson Dudley (1972). *Poverty, MacMillan Studies in Economics,* MacMillan, London.

Karmakar, K. G. (1999). *Rural Credit and Self-Help Groups, Micro-Finance Needs and Concepts in India*. Sage Publications, New Delhi.

Kaushik Dasu (1984). *The Development Economy: A Critique of Contemporary Theory,* Oxford University Press, Delhi.

Khan Azizur Rahman & Eddy Lee (1984). *Poverty in Rural Asia,* Asian Employment Programme (ARTEP), International Labour Organisation, Bangkok, Thailand.

Kuznets S. (1965). *Economic Growth and Structure,* Heinemann, London.

Lewis, A. (1966). *Developmnet Planning,* Allen & Unwin, London.

Mahammad Haan Khan (1981). *Underdevelopment and Agrarian Structure in Pakistan,* A West View Replica Edition, West View Press, U.S.A.

Maheswari, S. R.(1985). *Rural Development in India,* Sage Publications, Delhi.

Minhas R. S. (1974). *Planning and the Poor,* S. Chand & Company Limited, New Delhi.

Mukta Mittal (1995). *Women Power in India,* Anmol Publications Pvt. Ltd., New Delhi.

Myrdal Gunner (1968). *Asian Drama, Volume-III,* Twentieth Century Fund, New York.

NABARD (1999). *Banking with the Poor: Financing Self-help Groups,* CGM, NABARD, Hydreabad.

NABARD (1999-2000). *NABARD and Micro-finance,* Mumbai.

Nanda, Y.C. (2000). *Role of Banks in Rural Development in the New Millennium, National Bank for Agriculture and Rural Development,* Mumbai.

NCERT (2000). *Human Development in South India,* Oxford, New Delhi.

Parthasarathy, G. (1982). *Integrated Rural Development Concepts, Theoretical Base and Contradiction, in* "Development Planning and Policy", Edited by Gupta D.B., et al., Wiley Eastern, New Delhi.

Rahman, Hossain Zillus (1998). *Poverty Issues in Bangladesh,* Power and Participation Research Centre, Mimeo.

Rai & Tandon (1999). *Voluntray Development Organisation and Socio-economic Development,* Indian Economic Association, 82th Conference Volume, Amritsar.

Sakuntala Narasimhan (1999). *Empowering Women, An Alternative for Strategy from Rural India,* Sage Publications, New Delhi.

Sen A. K. (1984). Poverty and Famines: *An Essay on Entitlement and Deprivation,* Oxford University Press, Delhi.

Shylendra, H.S. (1999). *Promoting Women's Self-help Groups; Lessons from an Action Research Project of IRMA,* Anand, India, Working Paper No. 121.

The World Bank (2000-2001). *World Development Report,* Oxford, New York.

Todaro Michael, P. (1977). *Economics for a Developing World,* Longmans, London.

Todaro Michael, P. (1990). *Economics for a Developing World,* Second Edition, Longman, New York.

Von Braun, J., Bayes, F. and Akhter, R. (1999). *Village Pay Phones and Poverty Reduction. ZEF Discussion Papers on Development Policy No. 18,* Centre for Development Research, University of Barlin.

Von Pischke, J. D. et al. (1983) *Rural Financial Markets in Developing Countries: Their Use and Abuse,* John Hopkins University, Baltimore, U. S.A.

Yogesh Atal (1996). *Poverty and Participation in Civil Society,* Abhinav Publications, New Delhi.

Zeller, Manfred and Manohar Sharma (1998). *Rural Finance and Poverty Alleviation,* Food Policy Report, International Food Policy Research Institute, Washington DC, USA.

Journals

Amitava Mukherjee (1999). *Out of the abysis. The Challenge Confronting Some Civil Society Actors,* Indian Economic Association, 82 Conference, Amritsar.

Awasthi, P. K., et al., (1986). 'IRDP: Receptivity and Reaction', *Indian Journal of Agricultural Economics,* Vol. 41, No.4, October-December.

Bagchee Sandeep (1987). 'Poverty Alleviation Programmes in Seventh Plan: An Appraisal', *Economic and Political Weekly,* Vol. XXII, No. 4, January 24.

Bardhan, P K. (1973). On the Incidence of Poverty in Rural India of the Sixties, *Economic and Political Weekly,* February.

Bhat, Mazi, P. N. and et al., (1999). *Finding of National Family Health Survey, Regional Analysis, Economic and Political Weekly, Vol. XXXIV, Nos. 42 and 43,* Oct. 16-22/23-29.

Chambers, Robert (1994). *"Poverty and Livelihoods: Whose Reality Counts?" Overview Paper II, UNDP Stockholm Roundtable,* "Change: Social Conflict or Harmony?" 22-24 July.

Copertake Jemes G. (1996). *The Resilience of IRDP: Reform and Perpetuation of an Indian Myth. Development Policy Review,* 14

Dantwala, M. L. (1983). 'Rural Development: Investment Without Organisation', *Economic and Political Weekly.*

Desai, A. R. (1987). 'Rural Development and Human Rights in Independent India, *Economic and Political Weekly,* Vol. XXII, No. 31.

Desai, B.M. and J.W. Mellor (1993). *Institutional Fiance for Agricultural Development: An Analytical Survey of Critical Issues, Food Policy Review I,* International Food Policy Research Institute, Washinton, DC, USA.

Ghosh, D.K. (1995). *Group Cohesiveness in DWCRA Groups: An Application of Sociometric Approach,* Kurukshetra, May-June.

Govil, R.K. (1982). 'Micro-Level Planning and Rural Development', *Kurukshetra.*

Grewal, R.S. *et al.,* (1985). 'Impact of Integrated Rural Development Programme on Rural Women in Bhiwani District of Haryana', *Indian Journal of Agricultural Economics,* Vol. XL, No. 3, July-September.

Hare Gopal, G. & Balaramulu, Ch. 'Poverty Alleviation Programmes: IRDP in an Andhra Pradesh District, *Economic and Political Weekly,* Vol. XXIV, Nos. 35 & 36, September 2-9.

Hirway Indira (1984). *Programmes for Povety Eradication: A Critique of Target Group Approach,* Sardar Patel Institute for Economic and Social Research (Mimeo).

Jain, S.C. (1986). 'Poverty Alleviation Programmes in India: Some Issues of Micro Policy', *Indian Journal of Agricultural Economics,* Vol. XLI, No. 3, Conference Number, July-September.

Karmakar, K.G. (1999). *Rural Credit and Self-Help Groups; Micro-Finance Needs and Concepts in India,* Sage Publications, New Delhi.

Kumar Rajinder, *et al.,* (1986). 'Impact of Credit on Income, Employment and Capital Formulation of Rural Poor', *Indian Journal of Agricultural Economics,* Vol. 41, No.4, October-December.

M.S. Kallur (2001). *Empowerment of Women through NGOs: A Case Study of MYRADA Self-Help Groups,* Indian Journal of Agricultural Economics, Vol. 56, No.3.

Mosley, P. and R.P. Dahal (1985). *"Lending to the Poorest: Early Lessons from the Small Farmers: Development Programme, Nepal Development Policy Review,* Vol. 3, No. 2.

NIRD (1985). 'Employment and Income Generation Through IRDP, NREP and DRM', *Journal of Rural Development,* Vol. 4, No. 5, March-September.

Owusu, K. Opoku and William Tetteh (1982). *"An Experiment in Agricultural Credit: The Small Farmer Group Lending Programme in Ghana", Savings and Development,* Vol. 1, No. 1.

Rajaram Das Gupta (2001). *Working and Impact of Rural Self-Help Groups and Other Forms of Micro Financing, Indian* Journal of Agricultural Economics, Vol 56, No.3.

Rajasekhar, D. (1996), *"Problems and Prospects of Group Lending in NGO Credit Programme in India", Saving and Development,* Vol. 20, No.1.

Sinha, S.P. & Prasad Jagadish (1980). 'Special Programmes for Weaker Sections: An Evaluation', *Indian Journal of Agricultural Economics,* Vol. XXXV, No. 4.

Stiglitz, J.E. (1990) *"Paper Monitoring and Credit Markets",* The World Bank Economic Review, Vol. 4, No. 3.

Thakur, D.S. (1977). 'Rural Development in India: Past Experience and Tasks Ahead', *Indian Journal of Agricultural Economics,* Vol. XXXII, No. 3, July-September.

The Hindu 2002, 11th May 2002, Chennai.

Yaron, J. (1992). *Successful Rural Finance Institutions,* World Bank Discussion Paper, 150, Washington, DC, USA.

Reports

Amitava Mukherjee (1999). *Out of the Abysis, The Challenge Confronting Some Civil Society Actors,* Indian Economic Association, 82 Conference, Amritsar.

APDPIP (2002), *On Andhra Pradesh District Poverty Initiatives Project Appraisal Document (PAD), Report No. 20089,* South Asia Regional Office.

Chief Planing Officer (2002). *Hand Book of Statistics, Mahabubnagar District,* Mhabubnagar.

Chief Planning Officer Collectorate (2000). *Hand Book of Statistics, Krishna District,* Machilipatnam.

Chief Planning Officer Collectorate (2001). *Hand Book of Statistics, Chittoor District,* Chittoor.

CIRDAP (1998). *Increased Household Income and Rural Women in Asia, Impact on Status and Activities,*, Dhaka, Bangladesh.

CIRDAP (1998). *Poverty Gender and Participation,* Dhaka.

CIRDAP (1999). *Rural Development Report, Centre on Integrated Rural Development for Asia and Pacific,* Dhaka.

CIRDAP (2000). *Poverty Gender and Participation,* Dhaka.

CMIE (2000). *Profile of Districts, Economic Intelligence Service,* October, Mumbai.

Government of Andhra Pradesh (1998). *Annual Report of the Commission of the Rural Development,* Hyderabad.

Government of Andhra Pradesh (1999). *Annual Report of the Commission of the Rural Development,* Hyderabad.

Government of Andhra Pradesh (1999). *New Series on State Domestic Product,* A.P., Hyderabad.

Government of Andhra Pradesh (2001). *Provisional Population Totals, Series 29,* Hyderabad.

Government of Andhra Pradesh (2001). *Statistical Abstract,* Hyderabad.

Government of Andhra Pradesh (2001). *Strategy Paper,* Hyderabad.

Government of India (1991). *Census of India,* New Delhi.

Government of India (1997-2002). *IX Five Year Plan,* New Delhi.

Government of India (2001), *Provisional Population Totals,* New Delhi.

Government of India (1974). *Towards Equality—Committee on the Status of Women in India.*

Government of India (1998, 99), *Reports of the Commissioner of SC and STs,* New Delhi.

Haq. Mahbub Ul. (1997). *Human Development in South Asia,* Oxford University Press, New York.

Holcombe, Susan (1995). *Managing to Empower. The Grameen Banks' Experience of Poverty Alleviation,* Oxford University Press, Dhaka

IFAD (1996). *The State of World Poverty, Rome for a Discussion on the Process and Structural Causes of Poverty,* See Rovert Chambers (1983). Rural Development, Putting the Last First London, Longmans, One of the Best Discussions on how these Perpetuate Poverty.

IFAD (2001). *Rurual Poverty Report. The Challenge of Ending Rural Poverty,* Oxford, New York.

Indian Bank (2002-2003). *Annual Credit Plant, Krishna District (A.P.), Vijayawada.*

International Fund for Agricultural Development (IFAD) (1992). *The State World Rural Poverty—An Inquiry Into its Causes and Consequences,* New York University Press, New York.

ISACPA (1992). *Independent South Asia Commission for Poverty Alleviation.*

NABARD (1999). *Annual Report,* Mumbai.

NABARD (2000). *Annual Report,* Mumbai.

NABARD (2001). *Annual Report,* Mumbai.

NIRD (1994). *Rurual Development Report; Rural Employment,* Hyderabad, Andhra Pradesh.

NIRD (2001). *National Conference on SHG Movement in the Country & Swarnajanyanti Gram Swarozgar Yojana (SGSY), National Institute of Rural Development,* Hyderabad.

PEO (1985). *Evaluation Report on Integrated Rural Development Programme,* New Delhi.

RBI (1984). *Implementation of Integrated Rural Development Programme—* A Field Study.

SAARC (1992). *The Independent Source Asian Commission of the SAARC on Poverty Alleviation,* Dhaka.

South Asian Association for Regional Cooperation (SAARC) (1992). *Meeting the Challenge, Report of the Independent South Asian Commission on Poverty.*

The World Bank (1990). *World Development Report* Oxford, New York.

The World Bank (1991). *Gender and Poverty in India,* Washington DC.

The World Bank (1999-2000). *World Development Report 1999-2000,* Oxford University Press, New York.

UNDP (1994). *Human Development Report,* Oxford, New York.

UNDP (1996). *Human Development Report,* Oxford, New York.

UNDP (1997). *Human Development Report,* Oxford, New York.

UNDP (2000). *Human Development Report,* Oxford, New York.

World Bank (1990). *World Development Report—Poverty,* Oxford University Press.

Yerramaraju, B. and Firdausi, A.A. (1995). *Evaluation of DWCRA in Prakasam District,* Sponsored by Government of Andhra Pradesh, Administrative Staff College of India, Hyderabad.

Others

Government of Andhra Pradesh, Vision-2020, Hyderabad.

Government of India (1985). *Five Year Plan Documents (The Seventh and Eighth Five Year Plans 1985-95,* New Delhi, The Planning Commission).

NABARD (1984). *Study of Implementation of IRDP (Mimeo),* Bombay.

Government of Andhra Pradesh (1999). *Vision—2020,* Hyderabad, India.

Government of Andhra Pradesh, *Guidelines for Swarnajayanti Gram Swarozgar Yojana. Panchayati Raj and Rural Development Department,* Hyderbad.

IXth 5th Year Plan (1997-2000).

The Hindu (2002). April 27, Chennai.

The Hindu (2002). *Vision—2020.*

Index

F